WORK EFFECTIVELY IN ACCOUNTING AND FINANCE

WORK EFFECTIVELY IN ACCOUNTING AND FINANCE

Qualifications and Credit Framework

Level 2 Certificate in Accounting

British Library Cataloguing-in-Publication Data

A catalogue record for this book is available from the British Library.

Published by
Kaplan Publishing UK
Unit 2, The Business Centre
Molly Millars Lane
Wokingham
Berkshire
RG41 2QZ

ISBN 978-0-85732-210-4

Printed in Great Britain by WM Print Ltd, Walsall.

We are grateful to the Association of Accounting Technicians for permission to reproduce past assessment materials and example tasks based on the new syllabus. The solutions to past answers and similar activities in the style of the new syllabus have been prepared by Kaplan Publishing.

We are grateful to HM Revenue and Customs for the provision of tax forms, which are Crown Copyright and are reproduced here with kind permission from the Office of Public Sector Information.

CONTENTS

INTRODUCTION

HOW TO USE THESE MATERIALS

These Kaplan Publishing learning materials have been carefully designed to make your learning experience as easy as possible and to give you the best chance of success in your AAT assessments.

They contain a number of features to help you in the study process.

The sections on the Unit Guide, the Assessment and Study Skills should be read before you commence your studies.

They are designed to familiarise you with the nature and content of the assessment and to give you tips on how best to approach your studies.

STUDY TEXT

This study text has been specially prepared for the revised AAT qualification introduced in July 2010.

It is written in a practical and interactive style:

- key terms and concepts are clearly defined

- all topics are illustrated with practical examples with clearly worked solutions based on sample tasks provided by the AAT in the new examining style

- frequent practice activities throughout the chapters ensure that what you have learnt is regularly reinforced

ICONS

The study chapters include the following icons throughout.

They are designed to assist you in your studies by identifying key definitions and the points at which you can test yourself on the knowledge gained.

Definition

These sections explain important areas of Knowledge which must be understood and reproduced in an assessment

Example

The illustrative examples can be used to help develop an understanding of topics before attempting the activity exercises

Activity

These are exercises which give the opportunity to assess your understanding of all the assessment areas.

KAPLAN PUBLISHING

UNIT GUIDE

Working Effectively in Accounting and Finance consists of one unit.

Unit

2 credits

Purpose of the units

The AAT has stated that the general purpose of this unit is about gaining a range of transferable skills which will enable the learner to work effectively within an accounting environment. Learners will be able to work independently or as part of a team. It aims to prove a reasonable standard of literacy and numeracy skills which is essential for the workplace.

Learning outcomes

On completion of this unit the learner will be able to:

- Understand the accounting or payroll function within an organisation

- Demonstrate a range of effective communication skills

- Work independently or as part of a team

- Develop skills and knowledge to meet personal and organisational skills

Knowledge

To perform this unit effectively you will need to know and understand the following:

		Chapter
1	**Understand the accounting or payroll function within an organisation**	
1.1	Explain the role of accountancy or payroll and other financial functions within the business	1, 2
1.2	Identify the contribution of those in accounting or payroll and other financial roles to maintaining the smooth running, solvency and legal compliance of an organisation	1, 2
1.3	Identify your appropriate reporting lines within your working environment	7
1.4	Recognise and organisational policies and procedures that affect your work	3
2	**Demonstrate a range of effective communication skills**	
2.1	Demonstrate a level of numeracy and literacy skills appropriate to your role within the organisation	4
2.2	Present information in appropriate formats and within organisational guidelines for:	4

- Informal business report (including diagrams)
- Letter
- Email or memo

KAPLAN PUBLISHING

Delivery guidance

The AAT have provided delivery guidance giving further details of the way in which the unit will be assessed.

Understand the accounting or payroll function

Learners should be aware that the primary role of the staff of the accountancy, payroll and finance functions is to provide complete, accurate and timely information and support the other functions within the organisation.

Learners should be aware of the contribution the accountancy, payroll and finance functions make to the success of the organisation as a whole.

They need to understand that these functions play a vital role in ensuring the organisation remains solvent and to ensure that debts can be met. They will provide information to an organisation about the cash flow implications of its activities and when debts have to be repaid.

Learners need to be aware or the rules and regulations that exist and ensure fines and remedial work are minimised. The learner must understand that they need to follow procedures to protect theirs and others safety and security, ensure confidentiality is preserved and the procedures for the secure storage of data and information.

It is important that the learner is aware of reporting lines and understand that organisational policies and procedures influence many aspects of working practice.

Demonstrate a range of effective communication skills

The learner will be able to communicate effectively using business communications including informal business reports, letters, email and memos. Clear and concise communication creates greater efficiency in an organisation and learners are required to demonstrate numeracy and literacy skills which would be expected of a level 2 Accounting Technician. They may be required to use addition, subtraction, multiplication, division, percentages, fractions and rounding to a set number of decimal places.

The ability to produce informal business reports, letters, emails and memos is an important skill for the learner at this level. The production of hand written reports is assessable and they will need to be presented professionally.

Work independently or as part of a team

Learners will be required to demonstrate they have the necessary skills to work independently and manage their own workload effectively. Planning and prioritisation is important and learners may need to select the most appropriate planning aid.

Learners will be required to show how they meet deadlines and prioritise and how they keep their line manager informed.

Learners need to understand how their deadlines and efficiency affect other members of the team. Learners will understand their contribution to the team and the importance of meeting deadlines.

Conflict can occur in teams and learners need to understand when they can resolve a conflict of dissatisfaction and the circumstances when and to whom they have to refer issues which they cannot resolve. Learners must be able to suggest ways of resolving conflict.

Develop skills and knowledge to meet personal and organisational needs

Continuing Professional Development (CPD) is an important requirement of the accounting and payroll departments. The sources of CPD available and the requirement to record CPD must be fully understood.

Learners should know how to identify their own development needs and objectives on a formal basis and the need to include their manager in the process. It is important to be able to set clear SMART (specific, measurable, achievable, realistic, timely) objectives which are agreed with the manager. This process needs to be monitored and reviewed against performance criteria.

The effect of the development of staff skills and knowledge has on improving organisational efficiency and in helping to meet targets must be understood in order that CPD is seen by all as an investment rather than a burden.

THE ASSESSMENT

The format of the assessment

This is a skills unit where learners are required to demonstrate they have the skills to be able to work effectively in an organisation. Working practices will vary between organisations and as such learners will be required to demonstrate that these skills are transferable to all organisations. The AAT assessment for this unit will therefore normally be case study based to ensure that all learners whether currently working in an accounting environment or not will be able to demonstrate the necessary skills.

The assessment will be divided into 2 sections

Section 1 covers:

- Understand the accounting or payroll function within an organisation

- Work independently or as part of a team

Section 2 covers:

- Develop skills and knowledge to meet personal and organisational needs

Learners will be required to complete tasks, based upon a case study, some of which may require further research by the learner. The learner's completed answers to the set tasks will be presented for assessment in the form of a file as part of this unit is about communication, literacy and numeracy skills. The presentation of the finished work is extremely important and will be assessed as well as the content of the answers.

The assessment material will normally be provided by the AAT, delivered online and assessed locally. Learners will be required to demonstrate competence in both sections of the assessment.

Alternatively, with guidance and support from training providers learners can provide workplace evidence to be assessed locally by their training provider. The training provider will be required to ensure that all assessment criteria are covered.

STUDY SKILLS

Preparing to study

Devise a study plan

Determine which times of the week you will study.

Split these times into sessions of at least one hour for study of new material. Any shorter periods could be used for revision or practice.

Put the times you plan to study onto a study plan for the weeks from now until the assessment and set yourself targets for each period of study – in your sessions make sure you cover the whole course, activities and the associated questions in the workbook at the back of the manual.

If you are studying more than one unit at a time, try to vary your subjects as this can help to keep you interested and see subjects as part of wider knowledge.

When working through your course, compare your progress with your plan and, if necessary, re-plan your work (perhaps including extra sessions) or, if you are ahead, do some extra revision / practice questions.

Effective studying

Active reading

You are not expected to learn the text by rote, rather, you must understand what you are reading and be able to use it to pass the assessment and develop good practice.

A good technique is to use SQ3Rs – Survey, Question, Read, Recall, Review:

1 **Survey the chapter**

    Look at the headings and read the introduction, knowledge, skills and content, so as to get an overview of what the chapter deals with.

2 **Question**

    Whilst undertaking the survey ask yourself the questions you hope the chapter will answer for you.

3   Read

Read through the chapter thoroughly working through the activities and, at the end, making sure that you can meet the learning objectives highlighted on the first page.

4   Recall

At the end of each section and at the end of the chapter, try to recall the main ideas of the section / chapter without referring to the text. This is best done after short break of a couple of minutes after the reading stage.

5   Review

Check that your recall notes are correct.

You may also find it helpful to re-read the chapter to try and see the topic(s) it deals with as a whole.

Note taking

Taking notes is a useful way of learning, but do not simply copy out the text.

The notes must:

- be in your own words
- be concise
- cover the key points
- well organised
- be modified as you study further chapters in this text or in related ones.

Trying to summarise a chapter without referring to the text can be a useful way of determining which areas you know and which you don't.

Three ways of taking notes

1   Summarise the key points of a chapter

2   Make linear notes

A list of headings, subdivided with sub-headings listing the key points.

If you use linear notes, you can use different colours to highlight key points and keep topic areas together.

Use plenty of space to make your notes easy to use.

3   Try a diagrammatic form

The most common of which is a mind map.

To make a mind map, put the main heading in the centre of the paper and put a circle around it.]

Draw lines radiating from this to the main sub-headings which again have circles around them.

Continue the process from the sub-headings to sub-sub-headings.

Highlighting and underlining

You may find it useful to underline or highlight key points in your study text – but do be selective.

You may also wish to make notes in the margins.

Further reading

In addition to this text, you should also read the "Student section" of the "Accounting Technician" magazine every month to keep abreast of any guidance from the examiners.

The role of accounting and the supply of information

1

Introduction

This introductory chapter covers the purpose of information and the role of accounting within an organisation.

KNOWLEDGE

1.1 Explain the role of accounting and other financial functions within business.

1.2 Identify the contribution of those in accounting and other financial roles to maintaining the smooth running solvency and legal compliance of an organisation.

CONTENTS

1 The purpose of management information

2 The sources and categories of information

3 Management accounting and financial accounting

4 Responsibility centres

1 The purpose of management information

1.1 What is a manager?

A manager in an organisation can include anyone who is involved in the decision-making processes, and in the planning and controlling of the organisation's activities. There are different levels of management, for example the managing director is at a higher level than the line manager of the production department. The types of decision taken by each of these managers is very different, therefore the information requirements of the managers will be different. Managers need useful information (management information) in order to make decisions, to plan and to control the activities of the company. Financial and Management accountants provide managers with this information.

1.2 Decision making

In the course of running a business, management will be faced with many decisions. These will include both **long-term decisions** about the future direction of the business and **short-term decisions** about the day-to-day running of the organisation.

Examples of **long-term,** or strategic, decisions that managers may make include:

(a) which products to continue to produce and sell based upon factors such as the profitability and market share of those products

(b) which products to withdraw from manufacturing and selling

(c) how many staff to employ – whether there should be a reduction in the number of employees or whether more staff should be recruited

(d) whether or not to invest in new machinery and equipment.

Other **day-to-day** or operational decisions that might have to be made include:

(a) which products to make and the detailed scheduling of production activities

(b) how much overtime is required to meet output requirements

(c) how much inventory to hold, taking into account the cost of holding inventory compared with the cost of placing frequent orders and the risk of running out of inventory completely.

Data and information

Data consist of raw facts and statistics before they have been processed. Once data has been processed into a useful form, appropriate to the needs of the user, it is called **information**.

Useful management information enables managers to make **informed decisions**. This does not mean the managers will definitely make the right decisions or those that are necessarily the best for the business. Information is simply an aid to the decision-making process

1.3 Planning

The management of an organisation will spend much of its time looking forward and planning the longer-term operations and strategies of the organisation. In order to be able to plan how to operate successfully in the future, managers will need current, detailed information about the organisation.

Management will need to make detailed plans. These plans may include how many of each type of product to make and sell, what these products will cost to make, how many employees are required to make the products and how much they must be paid. These detailed plans are expressed in financial terms in the organisation's **budgets**.

In order to prepare these budgets, managers will need to know what each product costs to manufacture or how much it costs to provide a particular service to customers in order to decide which products or services to continue producing. They will need to know how productive the various employees or work groups are in order to concentrate efforts on improving productivity. They will need to know how much has been spent on advertising in the past in order to determine how much should be spent in the future.

1.4 Control

As well as making plans for the future management will also be concerned with whether the plans and budgets for the current period are being achieved. Regular comparison of actual costs and income with those that were anticipated in the budget for the period enables managers to identify where control action may be necessary. Control action might be taken in order to bring actual performance back into line with the budget, or if this is not possible then it may be necessary to prepare a revised budget. This new budget is then used to continue to exercise control, by regular comparison of the actual results with the revised budget.

1.5 The features of effective management information

For management information to be useful and effective it must have a number of qualities. Cost and management accounting information systems should be designed to produce information with all of the following desirable qualities although this may not be possible in all cases.

Relevant

The information must be relevant to the needs of the users. The provision of irrelevant information wastes time and money and there is a risk that relevant information might be overlooked if the manager is required to search for the relevant items.

- **Difficulty:** if there is a variety of users it can be difficult to identify the needs of each individual

Reliable

The information should be of a standard that can be depended upon by users when they are making their decisions.

- **Difficulty:** the complexities of modern business make reliability difficult to achieve in all cases

Understandable

The information should be understandable by the user. Excessive use of jargon must be avoided and the level of complexity of the information should be appropriate to the skill and knowledge of the manager who is using it.

- **Difficulty:** users may have differing levels of ability

Complete

The user must be provided with all the information necessary to make decisions and plan and control activities.

- **Difficulty:** there can be a conflict between completeness and relevance. It can be difficult to ensure completeness without overwhelming the user with too much information

Accurate

Linked to the requirement for reliability, information must be accurate otherwise incorrect actions might be taken based on inaccurate information.

- **Difficulty:** it is usually necessary to determine a *sufficient* level of accuracy. Depending on the type of information, perfect accuracy is not always possible or necessary. For example figures may be rounded to the nearest hundred or to the nearest thousand.

Timely

Information that is provided late will be less effective as any action based on the information may be taken too late.

- **Difficulty:** there can be a conflict between timeliness and accuracy. Information that is provided very rapidly will usually of necessity include a number of estimates

Clear

Information must be communicated in a way which is clear and easily understood by the user. For example tables should be used where appropriate.

- **Difficulty:** the differing ability levels of users of the information may mean that some can easily understand a technical diagram whereas other users of the information might require a longer, narrative explanation.

Consistent

The same principles should be applied in preparing consecutive management reports so that comparisons are possible between different periods.

- **Difficulty:** a focus on consistency might introduce an element of rigidity into the management reporting processes.

Cost effective

Management information is not effective if the cost of obtaining it is more than the benefits it is expected to provide. This point is linked to the need for *sufficient* accuracy and timeliness. Information that is perfectly accurate and which takes a long time to produce may be so expensive that its cost outweighs any savings or benefits derived from decisions based on that information.

- **Difficulty**: until the information is ready for use it can be difficult to determine whether it will generate sufficient benefits or savings to cover its cost

2   The sources and categories of information

Information may be based on primary data or on secondary data and may be obtained from internal sources or from external sources.

2.1   Primary data and secondary data

Primary data is gathered for a specific purpose. For example a company might interview its own customers directly to find out more about their buying habits.

Secondary data is not originally gathered for a single purpose but may be used in a variety of ways. For example instead of interviewing customers directly (gathering primary data) a company might use a secondary source of data such as published government statistics in order to investigate customer buying patterns.

2.2   Internal sources of information

Internal sources of information come from within the organisation itself, for example from the personnel records or from the financial accounting records.

Examples of internal information include the following:

- The rate of pay for employees with appropriate skills might be provided by the personnel department when a new product is being costed.

- In an accountancy firm detailed time records might be provided by the auditing department to assist in preparing invoices for audit work completed.

2.3   External sources of information

External information comes from sources outside the organisation.

Examples of external information include the following:

- Consumer price index statistics

- Health and Safety legislation

- Financial Reporting Standards.

3 Management accounting and financial accounting

Financial accounting information and **management accounting** information will both use the same basic data but they will be presented differently and will fulfil different roles.

3.1 Financial accounting

The **financial accounts** record transactions between the business and its customers, suppliers, employees and owners. The managers of the business must account for the way in which funds entrusted to them have been used and, therefore, records of assets and liabilities are needed as well as a statement of any increase in the total wealth of the business. Financial accounts are presented in the form of an **income statement** and a **balance sheet**.

Definition

Financial accounting is:

- the classification and recording of monetary transactions; and

- the presentation and interpretation of the results of those transactions in order to assess performance over a period and the financial position at a given date.

3.2 Cost accounting

Cost accounting involves applying a set of principles, methods and techniques to determine and analyse costs within the separate units of a business.

Definition

The establishment of budgets, standard costs and actual costs of operations, processes, activities or products; and the analysis of variances, profitability or the social use of funds.

3.3 Management accounting

Management accounting is a wider concept involving **professional knowledge and skill** in the preparation and presentation of information to all levels of management in an organisation. The source of such information is the financial and cost accounts. The information is intended to assist management in decision making and in the planning and control of activities in both the short and long term.

Definition

An integral part of management concerned with identifying, presenting and interpreting information which is used for formulating strategy, planning and control, decision making and optimising the use of resources.

3.4 involvement with management

Financial accounting, cost accounting and management accounting involve participation in management to ensure that there is effective:

- formulation of plans to meet objectives
- formulation of short-term operational plans
- acquisition and use of finance and recording of actual transactions
- communication of financial and operating information
- corrective action to bring plans and results into line
- reviewing and reporting on systems and operations.

3.5 Financial accounts and management information

It may be helpful to look at a simple income statement to see the role of management accounting:

XYZ Company

Income statement for period X

	£	£
Turnover		200,000
Cost of sales:		
Materials consumed	80,000	
Wages	40,000	
Production expenses	15,000	
		135,000
Gross profit		65,000
Marketing expenses	15,000	
General administrative expenses	10,000	
Financing costs	4,000	
		29,000
Net profit		36,000

This statement may be adequate to provide outsiders with an overview of the trading results of the whole business, but managers would need much more detail to answer questions such as:

- What are the major products and are they profitable?

- By how much has inventory of raw materials increased?

- How does the labour cost per unit compare with the cost for last period?

- Is the expenditure incurred by the personnel department higher than expected?

The management accounting system reports will provide the answers to these (and many other) questions on a regular basis. In addition, the management accounts will contain detailed information concerning raw materials inventory, work in progress and finished goods as a basis for the valuation necessary to prepare periodic and final accounts.

3.6   The relationship between cost and management accounts and financial accounts

Financial accounting information and cost and management accounting information come from the same sources but are presented differently. For example the cost of purchases for a week will be found in the financial accounting records from the purchases day book posted to the purchases account. The original information for the primary records would have come from the purchase invoices.

For management information purposes it may be more useful for the purchases of each different type of raw material to be identified. Again, the information will come from the purchase invoices but instead of a single total for purchases this will be broken down into each raw material.

For all of the different costs of a business the information that is recorded in the financial accounting records will be same as that recorded in the management accounting records. The only difference will be in the way in which the information is classified and presented.

The main differences between financial accounts and management accounts can be summarised in the following table.

Financial accounts	Management accounts
Limited companies are required by law to prepare them	Records are not mandatory
Accordingly, the cost of record-keeping is a necessity	Accordingly, the cost of record-keeping needs to be justified
Objectives and uses are not defined by management	Objectives and uses can be laid down by management
Mainly an historical record	Regularly concerned with future results as well as historical data
Information must be compiled prudently and in accordance with legal and accounting requirements	Information should be compiled as management requires, the key criterion being relevance
Prepared for external reporting	Prepared for internal use only

3.7   Cost accounting system

The cost accounting system is the **entire system of documentation**, accounting records and personnel that provide periodic cost accounts and cost information for management as part of the management reporting system.

3.8 Benefits of cost accounting and the accounting technician's role

The main benefit is the provision of information that can be used specifically to:

- disclose profitable and unprofitable activities
- identify waste and inefficiency
- analyse movements in profit
- estimate and fix selling prices
- value inventory
- develop budgets and standards to assist planning and control
- evaluate the cost effects of policy decisions.

Thus, by a **detailed analysis** of expenditure, cost accounting becomes an important element of **managerial planning and control**.

The accounting technician will have access to a large volume of information from the cost accounting records and will use this information to answer a wide variety of questions, for example:

- What is the cost of a particular product, service or department?
- What is the profitability of a certain product, service or department?
- Using the cost of a product or service, what selling price should be set?
- What is the value of inventory at the end of the period?
- What is the difference between the budgeted cost and the actual cost?

To summarise it can be said that Financial Accounting involves the recording of day to day transactions and the analysis of capital and revenue expenditure and income.

Through the maintenance of both the Sales and Purchase Ledgers a close control is kept upon the Debtor and Creditor balances.

Debtors' accounts are subject to internal controls in the form of credit control procedures that assure a managed flow of cash from debtors so that suppliers can be settled when due and other expenses can be paid on time.

These controls have a direct effect upon the cash flow of the business and thus its financial strength and solvency (its ability to pay its way).

Management Accounting is concerned with the allocation and control of resources. The Management Accountant forecasts the cash flow based on information from the financial accounting function. This would account not only for day to day revenue expenditure and income but future payments for capital expenditure, dividends and taxation including VAT.

This has an effect on the overall solvency of the business. The Management Accountant would also prepare longer term plans in the form of budgets.

4 Responsibility centres

4.1 What is a responsibility centre?

A responsibility centre is any part of an organisation for which the performance can be measured and whose performance is the direct responsibility of a specific manager. The type of responsibility centre that is used will depend on the level of control that the individual manager is able to exercise.

4.2 Cost centres

Definition

A **cost centre** is a production or service location, function, activity or item of equipment for which **costs** can be determined.

A **cost centre** is a responsibility centre to which costs can be related, for example, a paint manufacturer's cost centres might be:

- mixing department
- packaging department
- stores
- maintenance
- canteen
- administration
- selling and marketing departments.

The mixing department and the packaging department are **production** cost centres as the paint is actually produced and made ready for sale in these centres. The other responsibility centres are **service** cost centres as they support the production function and provide additional services required by the organisation.

For an accountancy practice, a service organisation, the cost centres might include:

- audit
- taxation
- accountancy
- word processing
- administration
- canteen
- various geographical locations e.g. the London office, the Reading office, the Edinburgh office.

Determining the costs for each cost centre is important for:

- relating costs to cost units, i.e. to the individual units of product or service produced
- planning future costs
- controlling costs, i.e. comparing either actual to budgeted, or actual to cost to 'buy in'.

Therefore, a **cost centre manager** is responsible only for the cost incurred in the centre.

4.3 Profit centres

> ### 🔍 Definition
>
> A **profit centre** is a production or service location, function or activity for which **costs and revenues, and therefore profit,** can be determined.

Thus a profit centre is a **responsibility centre** which is similar to a cost centre, but which has identifiable revenues as well as costs.

For a paint manufacturer profit centres might be a specific site or factory. For an accountancy practice the profit centres might be the individual locations or the type of business undertaken (audit, consultancy, accountancy, etc). Clearly all profit centres can also be cost centres, but not all cost centres can be profit centres.

Determining the excess of revenue over cost for each profit centre is important for:

(a)   planning future profits

(b)   controlling costs and revenues, i.e. comparing actual to budget

(c)   measuring management performance.

The **manager of a profit centre** is therefore accountable for costs, revenues and profit.

4.4   Investment centres

> ### 🔍 Definition
>
> An **investment centre** is a production or service location, function or activity for which **costs, revenues and net assets** can be determined.

Therefore an investment centre is similar to a profit centre but as well as having identifiable costs and revenues it also has identifiable assets and liabilities.

For our paint manufacturer this could be a group of sites or factories. For the accountancy practice the Edinburgh office and the London office.

An **investment centre manager** is therefore accountable for costs, revenues, profit and assets employed in the responsibility centre. The performance of an investment centre manager can be appraised according to the level of profit achieved in relation to the value of the assets or capital employed to earn that profit. We will return in a later chapter to look at this aspect of performance measurement in more detail.

The **manager of an investment centre** is therefore accountable for costs, revenues, profit and the level of investment in the centre.

4.5   The hierarchy of responsibility centres

Cost centres, profit centres and investment centres are often arranged in a hierarchy. There may be several cost centres within a single profit centre, several profit centres within an investment centre and several investment centres within the organisation as a whole.

5 Summary

This introductory chapter outlined the purpose and sources of information and how management uses this to achieve their objectives.

It distinguished between Financial and Management Accounting and how these functions aid the profitability and solvency of a business as a going concern.

The role and function of payroll accounting

2

Introduction

The role of payroll is a very important one in businesses. It is crucial that businesses pay employees on time and that the correct amount of tax is paid to HMRC.

KNOWLEDGE	CONTENTS
1.1 Explain the role of the payroll function within business.	1 Overview of the payroll function
1.2 Identify the contribution of those in payroll to maintaining smooth running, solvency and legal compliance of an organisation.	2 Gross pay
	3 Income tax
	4 National Insurance contributions
	5 Other deductions
	6 Payroll accounting procedures

1 Overview of the payroll function

1.1 The payroll system

The payroll system in a business is of utmost importance. The payroll staff not only have a responsibility to calculate correctly the amount of pay due to each employee but they must also ensure that each employee is paid on time with the correct amount and that amounts due to external parties such as HM Revenue and Customs are correctly determined and paid on time.

There are many facets to the payroll function and each will be briefly covered as an introduction in this section and then considered in more detail in later sections of the chapter.

1.2 Calculation of gross pay

The initial calculation that must be carried out for each employee is the calculation of the employee's gross pay. Gross pay is the wage or salary due to the employee for the amount of work done in the period which may be a week or a month depending upon how frequently the employees are paid.

Gross pay may depend upon a number of factors:

- basic hours worked;
- overtime hours worked;
- bonus;
- commission;
- holiday pay;
- sick pay.

1.3 Deductions

Once the gross pay for each employee has been determined then a number of deductions from this amount will be made to arrive at the net pay for the employee. Net pay is the amount that the employee will actually receive.

Some deductions are compulsory or statutory:

- Income tax in the form of PAYE;
- National Insurance Contributions (NIC).

Other deductions are at the choice of the employer or employee and are therefore non-statutory:

- Save as you earn;
- Give as you earn;
- Pension contributions.

1.4 Payment of wages or salaries

Once the net pay has been determined then each employee must be paid the correct amount, by the most appropriate method at the correct time.

1.5 Payments to external agencies

As you will see later in the chapter employers deduct income tax and NIC from each employee's wages or salaries and the employer must also pay its own NIC contribution for each employee. This is done by making payment to HM Revenue and Customs on a regular basis and this is therefore another responsibility of the payroll function.

1.6 Accounting for wages and salaries

Finally once the wages and salaries for the period have been paid then the amounts involved must be correctly entered into the ledger accounts.

1.7 Accuracy and confidentiality

Whilst carrying out all of these calculations and functions it is obviously important that the calculations are made with total accuracy. Not only is the amount that each individual will be paid dependent upon these calculations but there is a statutory duty to make the correct deductions from gross pay and to pay these over to HM Revenue and Customs.

Payroll staff deal with confidential and sensitive information about individuals such as the rate of pay for an individual. It is of the utmost importance that such details are kept confidential and are not made public nor allowed to be accessed by unauthorised personnel.

2 Gross pay

2.1 Introduction

Gross pay is the total amount payable to the employee before any deductions have been made. Gross pay can be made up of many different elements, e.g.

- normal wages or salary;
- overtime;
- shift payments;
- bonus;
- commission;
- holiday pay;
- statutory sick pay (or SSP); and
- statutory maternity pay (or SMP).

2.2 Wages and salaries

These are fairly straightforward. Employees will have an agreed monthly, weekly or hourly rate.

The monthly and weekly rates will not need any further calculations.

However, for hourly paid employees calculations will be needed for the total earnings. The source of this information might be clock cards.

Definition

A clock card is a card which records the hours worked by an employee.

As the employee arrives or leaves they put their card in the slot of a special clock. The mechanism inside the clock stamps the time on the card.

The payroll clerk would transfer the number of hours worked onto special calculation sheets.

2.3 Overtime and shift payments

These need to be identified so that the payroll clerk can calculate the amount payable.

Overtime is hours worked which are over and above the agreed number of weekly or monthly hours for that employee. For example, it may be agreed that an employee has a standard working week of 38 hours. If he works for 42 hours in a week then he has worked 4 hours of overtime.

Overtime or shifts worked might be recorded on:

- clock cards;
- timesheets; or
- authorisation forms (signed by the employee's supervisor).

Some employees are paid at a higher rate for overtime. They might be paid at one and a half times the normal rate. This is called time and a half.

Twice the normal rate is double time.

Some employees might be paid premium rates or bonuses for working certain shifts.

2.4 Bonus and commission payments

The business may pay certain employees a bonus. This bonus may be for achieving a particular target.

Company directors often receive a bonus if the company achieves certain profits.

Companies with a large number of sales representatives may pay their sales representatives a commission as part of their salary. This commission is based on the value of the sales they make.

For instance, a salesman might be paid a basic salary of £10,000 a year plus a 1% commission on sales that he makes.

2.5 Holiday pay

Most employers pay their employees even while they are on holiday.

If the employee is paid monthly, then there is no problem. The employee is paid the usual amount at the normal time.

If the employee is paid weekly, they would prefer to be paid for the holiday period in advance. This means that if the employee is taking two weeks' holiday they will have to be paid three weeks' wages at once.

2.6 Statutory sick pay (SSP) and statutory maternity pay (SMP)

For basic accounting you will really only need to be concerned about basic wages and salaries, overtime and bonus payments.

If there is a reference to SSP or SMP you will be told how to deal with it.

3 Income tax

3.1 Introduction

Everybody in the UK has a potential liability to pay tax on their income!

Individuals pay **income tax**. The rate of tax depends on the size of their income.

> **Q Definition**
>
> Income tax is a tax on individuals' income.

3.2 Tax-free income

Everybody is entitled to some tax-free income.

This tax-free sum is known as the personal allowance.

> **Q Definition**
>
> The personal allowance is an amount which an individual is allowed to earn tax-free.

3.3 How income tax is paid

Employees pay their income tax through the **PAYE** (or Pay As You Earn) **scheme**.

> **Q Definition**
>
> The PAYE scheme is a national scheme whereby employers withhold tax and other deductions from their employees' wages and salaries when they are paid. The deductions are then paid over monthly to HM Revenue and Customs by the employer.

Looking at tax alone, the main advantages of this scheme are:

- employees pay the tax as they earn the income;

- most people do not have to complete a tax return unless they have several different sources of income;

- employers act as unpaid tax collectors (this is a serious responsibility and they can be fined for mistakes); and

- the government receives a steady stream of revenue throughout the year.

Activity 1

Under the PAYE Scheme who pays over the income tax to the Collector of Taxes?

A   The employee

B   The employer

C   The government

D   The Inspector of Taxes

4   National Insurance contributions

4.1   What is National Insurance?

National Insurance is a state scheme which pays certain benefits including:

- retirement pensions;

- widow's allowances and pensions;

- jobseeker's allowance;

- incapacity benefit; and

- maternity allowance.

The scheme is run by HM Revenue and Customs.

The scheme is funded by people who are currently in employment.

Most people in employment (including partners in partnerships, and sole traders) who have earnings above a certain level must pay National Insurance contributions.

4.2 Types of National Insurance contributions

Both the employer and the employee pay National Insurance contributions.

(a) Employees' National Insurance contributions

The employer deducts National Insurance contributions from an employee's weekly wage or monthly salary, and pays these to HM Revenue and Customs. Income tax and National Insurance contributions are both taxes on income, but they have different historical origins and are calculated in different ways. Employees' National Insurance is now, however, similar to income tax in many respects, and is really a form of income tax with another name.

Like income tax, employees' NI contributions are deducted from pay. The amount of the contributions an employee pays is linked to his or her earnings, and is obtained by reference to National Insurance tables supplied by HM Revenue and Customs.

You are not required to know how to use NI tables.

(b) Employer's National Insurance contributions

In addition to deducting employees' National Insurance contributions from each employee's wages or salary, an employer is required to pay the employer's National Insurance contributions for each employee. The amount payable for each employee is linked to the size of his or her earnings.

Employer's National Insurance contributions are therefore an employment tax. They are not deducted from the employee's gross pay. They are an additional cost of payroll to the employer, paid for by the employer rather than the employee.

5 Other deductions

5.1 Statutory deductions

So far we have looked at two types of deductions which the employer has to make from their employee's gross pay **by law**. These are **income tax** and **National Insurance** contributions. These are statutory deductions.

5.2 Non-statutory deductions

The employee may also choose to have further deductions made from their gross pay. These include:

- superannuation (pension) payments.

- payments under the **save as you earn scheme**; this is a strictly governed scheme offered by some employers that allows you to save a regular amount each pay day. You would use this money to buy shares in the company at a later date.

- payments under the **give as you earn scheme**; this scheme allows employees to request that their employer withhold a certain amount from their salary and pay it over to a charity, on their behalf.

- other payments, e.g. subscriptions to sports and social clubs and trade unions.

5.3 Summary of deductions and payments

It is time to summarise what deductions the employer makes from the employee's gross salary, and to whom the employer makes the various payments.

To process the payroll an employer must, **for each employee**:

- calculate the gross wage or salary for the period;

- calculate the income tax payable out of these earnings;

- calculate the employee's National Insurance contributions that are deductible;

- calculate any non-statutory deductions;

- calculate the employer's National Insurance contributions.

The employer must then:

- make the payment of net pay to each employee;

- make the payments of all the non-statutory deductions from pay to the appropriate other organisations;

- pay the employee's PAYE, the employee's NIC and the employer's NIC to HM Revenue and Customs for all employees.

Example

John earns £12,000 per annum. His PAYE, NIC and other deductions and the employer's NIC for the month of May 20X4 are:

	£
PAYE	125
Employee's NIC	80
Contribution to personal pension scheme	50
Employer's NIC	85

Calculate:

(a)   John's net pay;

(b)   the cost to the employer of employing John;

(c)   the amounts to be paid to the various organisations involved.

Solution

			Paid by employer to:
Gross pay per month		1,000	
Less: PAYE	125		HMRC
Employee's NIC	80		HMRC
Personal pension	50		Pension company
	——		
		(255)	
		——	
Net pay		745	John
		——	
Employer's NIC	85		HMRC

(a)   John's net pay is £745.

(b)   The cost of employing John is (1,000 + 85) = £1,085.

(c)   The pension company is paid £50 by the employer.

   HM Revenue and Customs is paid £290 by the employer:

	£
PAYE	125
Employee's NIC	80
Employer's NIC	85
	——
	290
	——

Where there are many employees, the employer will pay the amounts calculated per (c) above for all employees to HM Revenue and Customs with one cheque.

 Payroll accounting procedures

6.1 Introduction

The accounting for wages and salaries is based upon two fundamental principles:

- the accounts must reflect the full cost to the employer of employing someone (which is their gross pay plus the employer's NI contribution);

- the accounts must show the creditor for PAYE and NIC that must be paid over to HM Revenue and Customs on a regular basis, usually monthly.

We therefore need two accounts, plus a third control account.

(a)   The wages expense account which shows the full cost of employing the staff.

(b)   The PAYE/NIC account which shows the amount to be paid to HM Revenue and Customs.

(c)   The wages and salaries control account which acts as a control over the entries in the accounts. There are different ways of writing up this control account, but the way used by AAT is to use this account to control the gross pay and deductions from the employees, plus employers' NIC.

6.2 Double entry

The double entry reflects these two fundamentals and uses three main accounts – the wages and salaries control account, the wages expense account and the PAYE/NIC account.

1   Dr   Wages expense account
         Cr Wages and salaries control account
    with the gross wages of the employees.

2   Dr   Wages and salaries control account
         Cr Bank account
    with the net wages paid to the employees

3   Dr   Wages and salaries control account
        Cr PAYE/NIC account

with those deductions made from the employees which are payable to the HM revenue and customs

4   Dr   Wages expense account
        Cr Wages and salaries control account

     Dr   Wages and salaries control account
        Cr PAYE/NIC account

with the employer's NI contributions

Example

The wages and salaries information for an organisation for a week is given as follows:

	£
Gross wages	34,000
PAYE deducted	7,400
NIC deducted	5,600
Net pay	21,000
Employer's NIC	7,800

Write up the relevant ledger accounts in the main ledger to reflect this.

Solution

Wages and salaries control account

		£			£
2	Bank account	21,000	1	Wages expense account	34,000
			4	Wages expense account (ers NIC)	7,800
3	PAYE/NIC account (PAYE)	7,400			
3	PAYE/NIC account (ees NIC)	5,600			
4	PAYE/NIC account (ers NIC)	7,800			
		41,800			41,800

Wages expense account

		£			£
1	Wages and salaries control	34,000			
4	Wages and salaries control				
	(ers NIC)	7,800	Bal c/d		41,800
		41,800			41,800

PAYE/NIC account

	£			£
		3	Wages and salaries control	7,400
		3	Wages and salaries control	5,600
Bal c/d	20,800	4	Wages and salaries control	7,800
	20,800			20,800
			Bal b/d	20,800

6.3 Commentary on the solution

(a) The wages and salaries control account controls the total gross wages plus the employer's NIC and the amounts paid to the employees, and other organisations (e.g.HM Revenue and Customs for PAYE and NIC). The total gross pay is taken from the company payroll as are the deductions. Assuming that the company payroll schedule reconciles and no errors are made when posting the payroll totals to the account, the account should have a nil balance.

(b) The wages expense account shows the total cost to the employer of employing the workforce (£41,800). This is the gross wages cost plus the employer's own NIC cost.

(c) The PAYE/NIC account shows the amount due to be paid over to HM Revenue and Customs, i.e. PAYE, employee's NIC plus the employer's NIC.

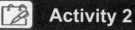 **Activity 2**

Given below is a summary of an organisation's payroll details for a week. You are required to prepare the journals to enter the figures in the main ledger accounts and to state the balance on the control account, once the net amount has been paid to the employees.

	£
Gross wages	54,440
PAYE	11,840
Employee's NIC	8,960
Employer's NIC	12,480

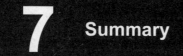 **Summary**

This chapter outlined the purpose and importance of the payroll function to the business.

It explained the constituents of both Gross and Net Pay by considering the elements of Statutory and Voluntary deductions and how through the financial accounting function these are accounted for.

When working in payroll it is essential to keep up with changes in legislation that effect the payment of wages and salaries.

Answers to chapter activities

Activity 1

B   The employer

Activity 2

1   Dr   Wages expense account
        Cr   Wages and salaries control account
with the gross wages of £54,440

2   Dr   Wages expense account
        Cr   Wages and salaries control account
with the employer's NI contributions of £12, 480

3   Dr   Wages and salaries control account
        Cr   PAYE/NIC account
with the PAYE of £11,840, and with the employee's NIC of £8,960
and with the employer's NIC of £12,480

Once the net amount to be paid to the employee has been posted by debiting the wages and salaries control account and crediting the bank account with £33,640, the balance on the control account will be nil.

Systems confidentiality, security and health and safety

3

Introduction

This chapter identifies some of the major risks to the security of computer systems and data, and discusses some controls available to reduce or eliminate those risks. The latter part of the chapter covers the issue of health and safety in the workplace from a general perspective and also the rules and regulations that all businesses must adhere to by law.

KNOWLEDGE	CONTENTS
1.4 Recognise any organisational policies and procedures that affect your work.	1 Security
	2 Protecting data from risks
	3 Legislative requirements for Data Protection
	4 Health and safety regulations for equipment
	5 Health and safety in your workplace
	6 Health and safety legislation and regulations

1 Security

1.1 Security risks

Security is defined by the British Computer Society as 'the establishment and application of safeguards to protect data, software and computer hardware from accidental or malicious modification, destruction or disclosure'.

There are five basic types of security risk to an organisation.

1. **Physical intrusion** leading to theft or damage of assets. Theft includes loss and illegal copying.

2. **Physical damage** to hardware or computer media – malicious damage, poor operating conditions, natural disasters and simple wear and tear can physically damage machinery and storage media such as disks, tapes and diskettes. These carry a triple threat – the cost of repair or replacement of hardware; the danger of damaged data or program files; and the cost of computer down time

   The loss of accounting records could be sufficient to cause the company to fail. Most non-technical users of systems would be surprised that there is an inherent risk to any computer system. Systems failure can mean that data is lost or physical damage can occur in a manner that is virtually impossible to guard against in a cost-effective way.

3. **Damage to data** – hackers, viruses, program bugs, hardware and media faults can all damage data files. The havoc caused by damaged data is made worse if it is not detected and rectified quickly. Hacking activities can:

   - generate information which is of potential use to a competitor organization

   - provide the basis for fraudulent activity

   - cause data corruption by the introduction of unauthorised computer programs and processing onto the system, otherwise known as 'computer viruses'

   - alter or delete the files.

4. Operational mistakes, due to innocent events such as running the wrong program, or inadvertently deleting data that is still of value to the organisation, can cause significant problems, ranging from the need to resuscitate files and repeat computer runs, to the possibility of losing customers. Links to the Internet bring extra security risks.

Examples include the following:

- corruptions such as viruses can spread through the network

- disaffected employees can do deliberate damage to data or systems

- hackers may be able to steal data or to damage the system.

- employees may download inaccurate information or imperfect or virus-ridden software from an external network

- information sent from one part of an organisation to another may be intercepted

- the communications link itself may break down.

5. Industrial espionage/fraud – can lead to loss of confidentiality with sensitive information being obtained by outsiders or non-related employees. Industrial espionage and sabotage can yield significant advantages to competitors, and fraud and blackmail is a significant threat.

1.2 Software security risks

The effects of poor security on software could be:

- **Deliberate physical attacks**, including theft or damage to installation in general – with files being taken. This threat can come from inside and outside the organisation e.g. access by unauthorised personnel could result in theft, piracy, vandalism.

- **Malicious damage** can also involve individuals from within or outside the organisation (such as hackers), damaging or tampering with data or information in order to disrupt the organisation's activity for malevolent reasons.

- **Fraudulent attacks** by employees or management or fraudulent transactions by altering programs. Fraudsters can divert funds from an enterprise to their own pockets or can attempt to hold employing companies to ransom by the threat of sabotage to vital computer systems.

- **Loss of confidentiality** – sensitive information obtained by outsiders or non-related employees.

1.3 Risks to information

The increasing use of computers in all aspects of business has led to a lot of information about individuals being kept by various organisations.

Information can be damaged, lost or stolen the same as equipment and other assets can. There are certain types of information that must be protected because of its confidentiality or value to competitors, for example:

- **Personal and private information** about employees and customers – there is a risk that some of this information is inaccurate which could cause serious problems for the individual concerned (e.g. being refused a loan if they have the wrong credit rating). The Data Protection Acts of 1984 and 1998 were introduced to help reduce this risk. The Acts stipulate that only legitimate parties can access data, and information must be secured against alteration, accidental loss or deliberate damage. Furthermore, the Act states that data must be obtained fairly, to precise specifications and must not be kept for longer than required. Individuals can find out information held about themselves by writing to the organisation and asking for a copy.

- **Critical information** about the business and its products/services, its marketing plans and legal or financial details of intended mergers, takeovers or redundancies. The importance of the organisation's commercial and trade information cannot be underestimated. The leaking of a company's trade secrets, such as its production processes, to its competitors may seriously affect its performance and its profits.

- Details related to the security of the organisation such as access codes, passwords and banking schedules.

There are also risks associated with copyright and copying, transmitting, sending and destroying confidential information without authorisation and appropriate security measures.

Remember email is neither secure nor confidential.

1.4   Computer viruses

> ### 🔍 Definition
>
> A **computer virus** is a piece of software that piggybacks on real programs and seeks to infest a computer system, hiding and automatically spreading to other systems if given the opportunity.

For example, a virus might attach itself to a program such as a spreadsheet program. Each time the spreadsheet program runs, the virus runs, too, and it has the chance to reproduce (by attaching to other programs) or wreak havoc. A computer virus passes from computer to computer like a biological virus passes from person to person.

Viruses can be classified using multiple criteria: origin, techniques, types of files they infect, where they hide, the kind of damage they cause, the type of operating system or platform they attack, etc.

A single virus, if it is particularly complex, may come under several different categories. And, as new viruses emerge, it may sometimes be necessary to redefine categories or, very occasionally, create new categories

Types of virus/infection include:

- **File infectors** – this type of virus infects programs or executable files (files with an .EXE or .COM extension).When one of these programs is run, directly or indirectly, the virus is activated, producing the damaging effects it is programmed to carry out. The majority of existing viruses belong to this category, and can be classified depending on the actions that they carry out.

- **Overwrite viruses** – this type of virus is characterised by the fact that it deletes the information contained in the files that it infects, rendering them partially or totally useless once they have been infected. Infected files do not change size, unless the virus occupies more space than the original file because, instead of hiding within a file, the virus replaces the file's content. The only way to clean a file infected by an overwrite virus is to delete the file completely, thus losing the original content.

- **E-mail viruses** – an e-mail virus moves around in e-mail messages, and usually replicates itself by automatically mailing itself to dozens of people in the victim's e-mail address book.

- **Trap doors** – undocumented entry points to systems allowing normal controls to be bypassed Logic bombs – are triggered on the occurrence of a certain event.

- **Time bombs** – which are triggered on a certain date e.g. Friday 13th.

- **Worms** – are not strictly viruses, as they do not need to infect other files in order to reproduce. They have the ability to self-replicate, and can lead to negative effects on the system and most importantly they are detected and eliminated by antiviruses.

- **Trojans** – are examples of malicious code, which unlike viruses do not reproduce by infecting other files, nor do they self-replicate like worms. They appear to be harmless programs that enter a computer through any channel. When that program is executed (they have names or characteristics which trick the user into doing so), they install other programs on the computer that can be harmful. A Trojan may not activate its effects at first, but when it does, it can wreak havoc on your system. They have the capacity to delete files, destroy information on your hard drive and open up a backdoor to your system. This gives them complete access to your system allowing an outside user to copy and resend confidential information.

Most computer viruses have three functions – avoiding detection, reproducing themselves and causing damage. The damage caused may be relatively harmless and amusing ('Cascade' causes letters to 'fall' off a screen), but are more often severely damaging.

The potential for the damage a virus can cause is restricted only by the creativity of the originator. Given the mobility between computerised systems and the sharing of resources and data, the threat posed by a viral attack is considerable.

Once a virus has been introduced, the only course of action may be to regenerate the system from back up. However, some viruses are written so that they lie dormant for a period, which means that the backups become infected before the existence of the virus has been detected; in these instances restoration of the system becomes impossible.

1.5 Fraudulent activities

Fraud is criminal deception – essentially it is theft involving dishonesty. It may be opportunistic or organised. The dishonesty may involve suppliers, contractors, competitors, other third parties, employees and ex-employees and, increasingly, organised crime and senior managers. Many frauds involve collusion and sophisticated methods of concealment. With an ever-increasing amount of business being carried out electronically (via 'e-commerce') the opportunities for cybercrime and computer fraud are also growing exponentially.

Fraud normally involves staff removing money from the company but other methods of fraud that might affect the data held on a computer system include:

- the creation of fictitious supplier accounts and submission of false invoices, usually for services rather than goods, so that payments are sent to the fictitious supplier

- corruption and bribery, particularly where individuals are in a position of authority as regards making decisions on suppliers or selecting between tenders

- misappropriation of incoming cheques from bona fide customers

- giving unauthorised discounts to customers

- stock losses, including short deliveries by driver

- fictitious staff on the payroll.

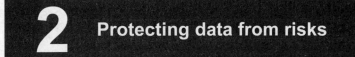

2 Protecting data from risks

2.1 Security measures

Computer security can be divided into a number of separate functions with different aims:

- **Threat avoidance:** this might mean changing the design of the system.

- **Prevention:** it is practically impossible to prevent all threats in a cost-effective manner.

- **Deterrence:** the computer system should try to both prevent unauthorised access, and deter people from trying to access the system. Controls to prevent and detect access include passwords and hardware keys. As an example, computer misuse by personnel can be grounds for dismissal.

- **Detection:** if the computer system is accessed without authorisation, there should be controls to sense the access and report it to the appropriate personnel. Detection techniques are often combined with prevention techniques. Controls will therefore include control logs of unauthorised attempts to gain access and manual reviews of amendments made to program and data files.

- **Recovery:** if the threat occurs, its consequences can be contained e.g. by the use of checkpoint programs. Procedures should be in place to ensure that if the computer system was destroyed, or compromised by a virus, then processing could continue quickly. A basic control procedure would be a complete backup of all data.

- **Correction:** any unauthorised changes made to the computer systems are corrected as soon as possible. This means that complete backups of all data are available and that staff are properly trained in the procedures necessary for recovery and re-installing of data in an emergency situation.

2.2 Physical security

Physical security includes protection against natural and man-made disasters, e.g. fire, flood, etc. Examples of measures to avoid physical damage to the system include:

- Fire precautions, e.g. smoke and heat detectors, training for staff in observing safety procedures and alarms

- Devices to protect against power surges.

Physical security also includes protection against intruders and theft. As computers and other hardware become smaller and portable, they are more likely to be taken from the organisation. Burglar alarms should be installed and a log of all equipment maintained. People with official access to the equipment who are taking it off-site should book it out with the appropriate authorisation.

Access to the building may be controlled by security guards, closed circuit TV monitoring access, other mechanical devices such as door locks and electronic devices, e.g. badge readers and card entry systems.

2.3 Data security

Guidelines for data security include keeping files in fireproof cabinets, shredding computer printouts if they include confidential information, controlling access to the data, (e.g. passwords and physical access controls) and taking back-ups of data to minimise the risks of destruction or alteration.

To offset the risk of fraudulent attacks there must be: adequate controls over input/processing/programs; strict division of duties; and regular internal audit review of systems and controls.

To prevent loss of confidentiality, there should be controls over input and output. With on-line systems there should be passwords issued only to authorised personnel, restricted access to files at the terminals and a computer log of attempted violations.

All disks containing important information must be backed up on a regular basis. Information on a computer is vulnerable: hard disks can fail, computer systems can fail, viruses can wipe a disk, careless operators can delete files, and very careless operators can delete whole areas of the hard disks by mistake. Computers can also be damaged or stolen. For these reasons backing up data is essential. This involves making copies of essential files, together with necessary update transactions, and keeping them on another computer, or on some form of storage media so that copies can be recreated. Master file copies should be taken at regular intervals and kept at locations away from the main computer installation.

Contingency plans for a disaster should include standby facilities, with a similar computer user or a bureau, being available to allow processing to continue.

2.4 Rules for using passwords

If passwords are used for authentication in a computer system, the safety of the access privileges will depend on their correct use and the following rules should be observed:

- It must not be possible to guess the password as easily as names, motor vehicle licence numbers, birth dates, or the like.

- The password should consist of at least one non-letter character (special character or number) and have at least six characters. The selection of trivial passwords (BBBBBB, 123456) must be prevented.

- Preset passwords (e.g. by the manufacturer at the time of delivery) must be replaced by individually selected passwords.

- The password must be kept secret and should only be known personally to the user.

- The password must be altered regularly, e.g. every 90 days. This will ensure that if an unauthorised person has obtained it, he or she will have limited use.

- The password should be altered if it has come to the knowledge of unauthorised persons.

- After any alteration of the password, previous passwords should no longer be used and reuse of previous passwords should be prevented by the IT system.

Activity 1

You have been asked for suggestions for a checklist of control procedures to remind authorised users about password security in the computer department.

2.5 Controls to help prevent hacking

Hacking is the gaining of unauthorised access to a computer system. It may form part of a criminal activity or it may be a hobby, with hackers acting alone or passing information to one another. Hacking is often a harmless activity, with participants enjoying the challenge of breaking part of a system's defences, but severe damage can be caused.

Once hackers have gained access to the system, there are several damaging options available to them. For example, they may:

- gain access to the file that holds all the ID codes, passwords and authorizations

- discover the method used for generating/authorising passwords

- discover maintenance codes, which would render the system easily accessible.

By specifically identifying the risks that the hacker represents, controls can be designed that will help prevent such activity occurring. Examples include:

- **Physical security** – check that terminals and PCs are kept under lock and key, and ensure that, where dial-in communication links are in place, that a call-back facility is used. (In call-back, the person dialling in must request that the system calls them back to make the connection.

- Management often requires that the contents of certain files (e.g. payroll) remain confidential and are only available to authorised staff. This may be achieved by keeping tapes or removable disks containing the files in a locked cabinet and issuing them only for authorised use.

- **Passwords** – the controls over passwords must be stringently enforced and password misuse should represent a serious disciplinary offence within an organisation. Associated with the password is a list of files, and data within files, which the user is allowed to inspect. Attempts to access unauthorised files or data will be prohibited by the operating system and reported at the central computer. For example, an order clerk using a VDU would be allowed access to the stock file, but not to the employee file. Similarly, the clerk would be allowed access to the customer file for purposes of recording an order, but would not be able to inspect details of the account. For systems that use passwords and logging on techniques, the workstation should not be left in the middle of editing. A screensaver with password control can be used for short absences, which saves closing down the machine.

- **Data encryption** – files can be scrambled to render them unintelligible unless a decoding password is supplied. Data may be coded so that it is not understandable to any casual observer who does not have access to suitable decryption software. Encryption provides a double benefit. It protects against people managing to gain access to the system, and it protects against the tapping of data whilst being transmitted from one machine to another.

- **System logs** – every activity on a system should be logged and be subject to some form of exception reporting, e.g. unusual times of access could be reported.

- **Random checks** – the 'constable on the beat' approach checks who is doing what at random intervals on the system, and ensures that they are authorised for those activities.

- **Shielding of VDUs** – to protect against people with detection equipment being able to view remotely what is being displayed on VDUs, the units may be shielded to prevent the transmission of radiation that can be detected

2.6 Preventative steps against computer viruses

It is extremely difficult to guard against the introduction of computer viruses. Even seemingly harmless screen savers have been known to contain deadly viruses that destroy computer systems. You should not download from the Internet or open e-mails that have attachments unless you know the source of the e-mail and that you trust that source. If you are in doubt you should ask your line manager for permission to open documents.

Steps may be taken to control the introduction and spread of viruses, but these will usually only be effective in controlling the spread of viruses by well-meaning individuals. The actions of hackers or malicious employees are less easy to control. Preventative steps may include:

- anti-virus software to prevent corruption of the system by viruses. Although the focus of the program is to detect and cure known viruses; it will not always restore data or software that has been corrupted by the virus. As new viruses are being detected almost daily, it is virtually impossible for the virus detection software to be effective against all known viruses

- control on the use of external software (e.g. checked for viruses before use)

- use of only tested, marked disks within the organisation

- restricted access to floppy disks and CDs on all PCs/workstations

- passwords and user numbers can be used to limit the chances of unauthorised people accessing the system via the public communications network.

3 Legislative requirements for Data Protection

3.1 Introduction

Several Acts of Parliament, notably the Data Protection Act 1998, the Copyright, Designs and Patents Act 1988 and the Computer Misuse Act 1990 regulate the use of computers. Each Act identifies a number of prohibited actions, which if proven in a court of law may lead the perpetrator to face damages and/or a fine or imprisonment or both. Additionally, the use of software may also be subject to the terms of licensing agreements entered into by the organisation you work for, which are enforceable in the civil courts.

3.2 Data Protection Act 1998

People have been keeping records for centuries and it might be considered surprising that concern is only recently being voiced. It is mainly because of the amount of information that can be gathered and stored and the ease with which that information can be manipulated and exchanged. School records, banking records, itemised telephone bills, medical records, etc, are all now capable of being consolidated to show what purchases someone makes, where they travel, who they talk to and how well they are. It is well known that information is traded for mailing lists.

The exchange of information itself is not worrying. The concern lies in the use made of the information, or how it may be interpreted. It may be used to decide whether to give a person a job, or given credit or called to the police station for interrogation.

The 1998 Data Protection Act covers how information about living identifiable persons is processed and used. It is much broader in scope than the earlier 1984 act, in that ALL organisations that hold or process personal data MUST comply. This Act has implications for everyone who processes manual or electronic personal data. It applies to filing systems of records held on computer or manual sets of accessible records e.g. a database of customer names, addresses, telephone numbers and sales details.

Under the terms of the Act, the need for privacy is recognised by the requirements that all data should be held for clearly designated purposes. Accuracy and integrity must be maintained and data must be open to inspection. Only legitimate parties can access data and information must be secured against alteration, accidental loss or deliberate damage. Furthermore, the Act states that data must be obtained fairly, to precise specifications and must not be kept for longer than required. It reinforces the need for confidentiality in business dealings. A business should not reveal information about one customer to another or information about its employees without their permission. The Act gives a data subject, with some exceptions, the right to examine the personal data that a data controller is holding about him or her. Individuals may write to a data controller to ask whether they are the subject of personal data, and they are entitled to a reply.

The data controller may charge a nominal fee for providing the information, but is required to reply within a certain time.

Where personal data is being held, the data subject has the right to receive details of:

(i)   the personal data that is being held

(ii)   the purposes for which the information is being processed

(iii)   the recipients to whom the information might be disclosed.

The data subject is also entitled to receive this information in a form that can be understood. In practice, this usually means providing the data subject with a printout of the data, and an explanation of any items of data (such as codes) whose meaning is not clear.

Any individual who suffers damage as a result of improper use of the data by the data controller is entitled to compensation for any loss suffered.

The *Data Protection Registrar* keeps a register of companies who hold information on computer. Each company that falls into this category must register of its own accord. A copy of the Data Protection Register is held in all major libraries.

Any unregistered data user who holds personal data that is not exempt commits a criminal offence; the maximum penalty for which is an unlimited fine.

3.3   Retention of documents

All businesses need to keep certain records for legal and commercial reasons. The difficulty lies in knowing which documents must be kept and for how long. Your organisation will have a policy that states the retention (and disposal) policy for such documentation. It will outline minimum retention periods for different types of documents based on best practice and, where applicable, the minimum retention periods required by law. The Data Protection Act stipulates that personal data is kept securely and that it should be accurate.

Business records are normally stored for at least six years. Payroll data must be kept for three years. There are a number of legal reasons why financial data, which of course includes personal data, should be kept for this time. Accounting records need to be kept for at least six years in case they are required as evidence in a legal case. They should also be kept so that they can be inspected by HM Revenue and Customs (formerly called the Inland Revenue or HM Customs and Excise) in case there is a tax or VAT inspection.

Once information becomes out of date, it may be deleted or destroyed but you must be aware that throwing a piece of paper in the waste bin is not destroying it. Even when information is out of date it may still be damaging if it falls into the wrong hands.

📝 Activity 2

A well-known customer telephones you and asks if you can look up on your screen and let him know if Joe Bloggs (another customer) is paying on time because he is having trouble getting money out of him and wonders whether he is going bust. Unfortunately, you know from your work that Joe Bloggs is not very good at paying his invoices. What should you say?

3.4   Patent and copyright infringement

Copyright law covers books of all kinds, sound recordings, film and broadcasts, computer programs, dramatic and musical works. Copyright in general terms is the right to publish, reproduce and sell the matter and form of a literary, musical, dramatic or artistic work. The **Copyright Designs and Patents Act 1988** states that the copyright holder has the exclusive right to make and distribute copies. The Copyright (Computer Software) Amendment Act 1989 indicates that software is treated as literary work and provides the same protection to the authors of computer software as it does to literary, dramatic and musical works. An amendment to the

1988 Act made in 1992 allows you to make a copy for back-up purposes. The Act makes it illegal to steal or to create copies of software. You are not allowed to make copies of software; make copies of manuals or allow copies to be made unless you have a licence from the owner of the copyright. It is also an offence to run the software on more than one computer at the same time unless that is covered in the licence.

Application packages will always contain an embedded serial number. If a pirate copy is found, the original purchaser can usually be determined.

There are steep penalties for companies prosecuted for software theft – unlimited damages, legal costs and the cost of legitimising the software. However, most breaches of copyright law happen because business users do not know what the law is.

Where a package is intended for use by more than one person, for instance on a network, then a multi-user licence is normally purchased, and this sets a limit on the total number of users. An alternative to this is a site licence, but this can be restrictive if, say, a travelling salesperson or someone working from home connects to the network. Some software can be copied legally; this is shareware. The software can be loaded onto a computer and tested; however, if the user decides to keep the software, then a royalty payment is due to the author. Freeware is software that can be copied and used without charge, although the software author retains the copyright to that software. Finally, public domain software is freely available and sharable software that is not copyrighted.

Modern software packages are complex and costly to produce, but are often easy to copy and distribute. Manufacturers are increasingly bringing prosecutions to try to reduce the number of pirate copies of their software. Staff should be made aware of this. Master and back-up copies of packages (usually on diskette or CD-ROM) should be kept in a locked safe. Programs on LAN servers should be given 'execute only' protection to prevent them being copied, and physical access to the server should be restricted. Regular and automatic audits should be made of personal computers to check that they only contain authorised programs.

3.5 Why worry about copyright rules?

The 'moral' reasons for following copyright rules are:

- copyright protection is essential to ensure that authors and publishers receive appropriate remuneration for their work

- acknowledging source and ownership of materials is good academic practice.

The pragmatic reasons for following copyright rules are:

- breaches of copyright can lead to civil prosecution and fines and, in worst cases, criminal prosecution

- licensing bodies make regular checks on certain organisations to ensure rules are being followed.

Note also, that you can infringe copyright, and be prosecuted, not only for making illegal copies yourself, but also as an 'accessory' by providing resources or authorisation (e.g. within a company) for someone else to illegally copy or perform material.

3.6   Computer misuse

Data that has been stored on a computer is, potentially, easier to misuse than that stored on paper. Computer-based data can be altered without leaving an obvious trace that it has changed. For example, an exam score written in a mark book can be changed but you can usually tell that the mark has changed. A mark stored on a computer can be changed and it will look as if nothing has happened.

Malicious (harmful) programs can be introduced to a computer that can damage the data stored on it; copy the data and send it somewhere else; or simply change the stored data. The programs are named after the way they get onto different computers: viruses, worms and Trojan horses.

It is very easy to make copies of computer data without leaving a trace that it has been done. A photocopier will also make copies of paper-based data but electronic copies of data can be smuggled out easily on floppy disks, memory chips or over a network connection.

Many computers are connected to a network or the Internet. If someone is persistent enough it is possible to use this connection to gain access to the computer (and the data on it) from outside. Of course, someone is able to physically break into a room and read data from paper records, however, it is sometimes more difficult to trace someone who has broken into a computer over a network or the Internet.

The Computer Misuse Act 1990 makes it a criminal offence to attempt to access, use or alter any computer data, program or service to which you have not been granted authorised access rights. Therefore any attempt to interfere with or bypass the security controls, to attempt to obtain information such as other people's password, or accessing or modifying other people's programs or files without permission are offences under the Act. Amongst other things, this Act makes illegal the activity of hacking and the introduction of viruses and worms.

The Act has created three new criminal offences.

(i)   **Unauthorised access** – This refers to any hacker who knowingly tries to gain unauthorised access to a computer system. The crime is committed in attempting to gain access, regardless of whether the hacker is successful or not. It includes: using another person's identifier (ID) and password; creating a virus; laying a trap to obtain a password; or persistently trying to guess an ID and password.

(ii)   **Unauthorised access with the intention of committing another offence** – This crime carries stricter penalties than the crime mentioned above. It seeks to protect against unauthorised entry with the intention of committing a further criminal act such as fraud.

Examples include: gaining access to financial or administrative records: reading or changing confidential information.

(iii) **Unauthorised modification of data or programs** – This makes the introduction of viruses into a computer system a criminal offence. Guilt is assessed upon the intention to disrupt or in some way impair the normal operation and processes of the computer system. Examples include: destroying another user's files; modifying systems files; introducing a local virus; introducing a networked virus; or deliberately generating information to cause a system malfunction.

3.7 Enforcement of standards

Observance of standards is more a matter of attitude than policing. When people are aware of the purposes of standards, they are more likely to follow them than if they are just threatened. Training is the main element of enforcement. There are some cases where ignoring standards should automatically lead to disciplinary action:

(i) any standards to do with safety, e.g. dangerous positioning of cables, particularly power cables, or working alone in an electrically hazardous environment

(ii) standards with legal implications, e.g. ignoring a requirement of the Data Protection Act or using an illegal copy of a program

(iii) actions which may affect a number of other people, e.g. running a program which might introduce a virus into a network

(iv) attempted unauthorised entry, e.g. trying to find someone else's password or unauthorised copying of confidential files (e.g. salaries).

4 Health and safety regulations for equipment

4.1 The Health and Safety (Display Screen Equipment) Regulations 1992

Ensuring the workplace is safe and healthy for employees can sometimes lead to emphasis on the obvious hazards such as lifting and use of dangerous equipment. However, the health and safety implications of poorly designed workstations is extremely important in today's environment where more and more people are working at personal computers and desks for long periods of time.

In addition to the Workplace (Health, Safety and Welfare) Regulations there are the Health and Safety (Display Screen Equipment) Regulations, which relate directly to use of display screen equipment (DSE). In general these are in place to ensure that workstations and jobs are well designed for individuals and that the risks to health and safety are minimised. The regulations do not cover screens whose main purpose is to show television or film pictures. Workstation equipment includes:

* display Screen Equipment (DSE) e.g. Computers, Terminals and accessories such as printers

* desks

* chairs

* accessories – e.g. telephone, foot rests, document holders, wrist rests

* work environment and work organisation.

The Health and Safety (Display Screen Equipment) Regulations 1992 came into effect from January 1993 to implement an EC Directive. They require employers to minimise the risks in VDU work by ensuring that workplaces and jobs are well designed.

The Regulations apply where staff habitually use VDUs as a significant part of their normal work (three hours or more per day) – even if they work from home. Other people, who use VDUs only occasionally, are not covered by these Regulations, but their employers still have general duties to protect them under other health and safety at work legislation.

4.2   Hazards

There are hazards associated with the use of Display Screen Equipment (DSE). They include:

* upper limb disorders (musculoskeletal disorders) – aches and pains in the hands, wrists, arms, neck, shoulders, back, etc

* visual difficulties – eyes can become tired and existing conditions can become more noticeable

* repetitive strain injury (RSI) – appears to arise from making the same movements repeatedly and affects your hands and arms

* fatigue and stress

* headaches

* skin irritation

* back and neck strain.

The likelihood and extent of these harmful outcomes is related to the frequency, duration, pace and intensity of the tasks; the adequacy of the equipment and its arrangement; the physical environment; the workplace's organisational 'climate'; the characteristics of the individual; the posture of the user; and other factors.

It should be noted, however, that only a small percentage of users will experience problems as a result of DSE. Those problems that do occur are generally not due to the equipment itself but the way it is used. The majority of concerns can be prevented by effective workplace and job design, ensuring that workstations and work patterns are designed to suit the individual.

4.3 Problems with Display Screen Equipment (DSE)

If you are a user of display screen equipment:

- Problems with the task, the workstation or its environment that are increasing the risk to your health and safety, and that you cannot resolve yourself, must be reported to your manager.

- You might experience the early signs and symptoms of ill health and identify the cause and the preventative measures to prevent continuing ill health. You must report this to your manager to enable support to be given for the measures you are taking.

- Ill-health problems might have developed to a stage that causes suffering and incapacity from doing all or part of your normal work. This will need to be the subject of an Accident Report. The manager's investigation into the accident may need the assistance of a Display Screen Equipment assessor. A long-term remedy might be identified and a short-term adjustment to task, routine and/or workstation might be appropriate. A DSE assessor is not competent to diagnose health conditions or advise on treatment or therapy. If however your doctor recommends certain adaptation of the task or workstation to your condition the assessor might be able to help with implementation.

- In more serious cases the condition might be such that the manager will need to arrange a rehabilitation programme and 'reasonable adjustments' of the work and workstations.

5 Health and safety in your workplace

5.1 The importance of health and safety at work

Of course, health and safety not only relates to computer screen equipment but to the workplace in general. The maintenance of safe working conditions and the prevention of accidents are most important. Top of your list of importance is obviously to protect yourself and others from dangers that might cause injury or sickness.

Health and safety is as important in an office as in a factory. Constant absenteeism through poor working conditions or accidents is costly for any organisation and people do not work as productively if they are ill, tired or in an unsatisfactory environment. It is therefore in the organisation's interests, as well as the employees', that health and safety procedures are observed. The costs of not having adequate measures to ensure health and safety include the following:

- Cash, cheques, equipment, machinery and stock may be destroyed or damaged. If the losses are serious the organisation may have to close down for a time. It may not be possible to complete orders on time, leading to a loss of customers and the consequent effect on profits and jobs.

- There may be serious injury to employees, customers and the general public, which could lead to claims for compensation and damage to the prestige of the organisation.

- Confidential records (e.g. correspondence and information on creditors, debtors and stock) may no longer be available.

Because health and safety at work is so important, there are regulations that require all of us not to put others or ourselves in danger. The regulations are also there to protect the employees from workplace danger.

6 Health and safety legislation and regulations

6.1 The basic requirements

Health and safety in the workplace is mainly a matter of common sense but, of course, none of us is entirely sensible all the time. This means that we need to have policies, procedures and rules about making our workplaces safe and healthy so that we are not put at risk whilst working.

The basis of British health and safety law is the Health and Safety at Work etc Act 1974, which is enforceable by law. It provides the legal framework to promote, stimulate and encourage high standards. The Health & Safety Executive and Environmental Health Officers check to make sure that all the regulations currently in force are being complied with by employers and the self employed, so far as is reasonably practicable.

The Act sets out the general duties that employers have towards employees and members of the public, and employees have to themselves and to each other.

The provisions of the Act place a duty on the employer to take all reasonable and practicable steps and precautions to provide a working environment that is safe and free from health hazards. Such steps and provisions should include information regarding the employee's work procedures, operations and general environment and the promoting of instruction, training and supervision. The employer has an obligation to ensure that an employee follows recognised safety codes of practice and is not endangering himself/herself and/or other employees.

Your employer has a duty to provide the following:

- safe ways in and out of the place of work

- a safe working environment

- safe equipment and procedures

- arrangements for the safe use, handling, storage and transport of articles and substances

- adequate information, instruction, training and supervision

- adequate investigation of accidents.

Failure to do so could result in a criminal prosecution in the Magistrates Court or a Crown Court. Failure to ensure safe working practises could also lead to an employee suing for personal injury or in some cases the employer being prosecuted for corporate manslaughter.

Your employer must also take out Employer's Liability Insurance and display the insurance certificate on the premises. This insurance will cover the employer for any accidents you might have at work.

But it is not only the employer who has a responsibility to make the workplace safe; the employee also has a responsibility to follow the safety rules and to protect both themselves and their colleagues from getting hurt. In some circumstances employers and employees can be prosecuted if they cause an accident by not following the health and safety regulations.

You as an employee (or a self-employed person) must:

- take care of your own health and safety in the workplace and not endanger the people you work with

- co-operate with anyone carrying out duties under the Act (including the employer)

- make sure you know what the health and safety rules of your employer are and keep these rules

- correctly use work items provided by your employer including personal protective equipment in accordance with training or instructions, and

- never interfere with or misuse anything provided for your health, safety or welfare.

As you can see, your employer has a duty to provide a safe working environment, but you, the employee, have a duty to look after yourself and other people within that environment.

7 Summary

This chapter focused on two important issues the security of information and data and elements of health and safety. These influence organisational procedures as business must adhere to various legislation that has an effect upon the workplace and those engaged in the business activity.

Answers to chapter activities

Activity 1

Some of the suggestions that would be included in a checklist for password security are:

- Passwords are meant to be secret and not revealed to anyone else.

- Never write it down.

- Change your password regularly or if you suspect someone knows it.

- Do not choose an obvious password such as your name, or in the case of a PIN, your date or year of birth.

- Try to avoid onlookers seeing you key in your password.

- For keyboard passwords, choose keys that require both hands rather than one or two finger, easy runs along a pattern of the keys.

Activity 2

You should not divulge any confidential information about your customer Joe Bloggs. Apart from it being very unprofessional it would also be breaking the law. Under the Data Protection Act 1998 data should not be made available to outsiders without authorisation.

Comparison and communication of information

4

Introduction

In this chapter we will be dealing with comparisons of current actual costs with information from different sources. We must consider where the information for comparison comes from and how to make meaningful comparisons. It will also consider the most common methods of reporting.

KNOWLEDGE
2.1 Demonstrate a level of numeracy and literacy skills appropriate to your role.
2.2 Present information in appropriate formats and within organisational guidelines for: Informal reports, letters, emails and memos.

CONTENTS

1 Comparisons required

1.1 Previous periods

In some cases you will be required to compare current costs and income to the same costs and income from previous periods in order to determine any significant differences. The previous period's costs and income will have been summarised in management cost reports and you need to be able to find these reports in your organisation's filing system.

1.2 Corresponding periods

In some businesses the income and costs tend to be seasonal and therefore a comparison of one period to another will not be particularly meaningful. For example in a retail business the period just before Christmas may be unusually busy therefore a comparison of income between December and November may not give any useful information. However in such cases it may be more useful to compare one period to the corresponding period of the previous year. In the case of the retailer the figures for December could usefully be compared to those of the previous December.

Another way in which comparisons can usefully be made with a corresponding period is by comparing the year to date costs or income to the same cumulative period in the previous year.

Again the figures for the historic information should be available from past management cost reports which will be kept in the filing system.

1.3 Budgets

You may also be required to compare current costs and income to the amounts that were budgeted for this period. Again you will need to be able to find the relevant budgets in the organisation's filing system.

2 Current period figures

In order to carry out the required comparison it will be necessary to find the correct current figures. These may be found from management reports such as coding listings or from the cost bookkeeping ledger accounts.

KAPLAN PUBLISHING

2.1 Coding listings

The coding listings are listings of all of the costs or income for a period which have been allocated to each cost centre or profit centre. In some cases the coding listing may need to be updated to take account of the most recent figures before they can be used for comparison.

Example

	£
021113	1,241
021114	883
021115	1,235
022113	512
022114	463
022115	987

You are also given the opening balances on the cost centre accounts which is the year to date apart from the last week in September:

Code	Year to date	Update	Closing balance at 30 September
	£	£	£
021113	31,236		
021114	145,346		
021115	23,875		
022113	65,489		
022114	7,235		
022115	12,345		

You will now need to update the opening figures in order to find the current year to date figures to use for comparison.

Code	Year to date	Update	Closing balance at 30 September
	£	£	£
021113	31,236	1,241	32,477
021114	145,346	883	146,229
021115	23,875	1,235	25,110
022113	65,489	512	66,001
022114	7,235	463	7,698
022115	12,345	987	13,332

☀ Example

A business has the following cost code structure.

For costs the first three digits denote the cost centre that has incurred the cost:

| Factory | 001 |
| Packaging | 002 |

The last three digits indicate the type of cost.

Materials	001
Labour	002
Expenses	003

The code for input VAT is 006230.

The business has received the following three invoices in the final week of September 20X7.

INVOICE

ABC STEELS LIMITED
25 Minshing Road
Leicester L1 6PW
To: Barts Fabricators Limited
37 Nestor Street
Birmingham BR2 7EZ

VAT registration: **315 6791 56**
Date/tax point: **27 September 20X7**
Invoice number: **39576**

Description of goods/services	Total (£)
20,000 kg steel tube	23,500.00
VAT @ 17.5%	4,112.50
Total	**27,612.50**

INVOICE

XYZ LIMITED
276 Albourgh Place
Manchester M27 8JU
To: Barts Fabricators Limited
37 Nestor Street
Birmingham BR2 7EZ

VAT registration: 23 576 89
Date/tax point: 26 September 20X7
Invoice number: 236785

Description of goods/services	Total (£)
100 packs cardboard packaging	2,700.00
VAT @ 17.5%	472.50
Total	**3,172.50**

INVOICE

PRIME TALK LIMITED
345 Carbury Business Park
Leicester L1 6YT
To: Barts Fabricators Limited
37 Nestor Street
Birmingham BR2 7EZ

VAT registration: 367 456 98
Date/tax point: 28 September 20X7
Invoice number: 3458

Description of goods/services	Total (£)
Telephone installation to factory	4,500.00
VAT @ 17.5%	787.50
Total	**5,287.50**

Code	Year to date	Update	Closing balance at 30 September 20X7
	£	£	£
001001	254,867.00		
001002	23,456.00		
001003	15,345.00		
002001	25,346.00		
002002	7,345.00		
002003	5,675.00		
006237	7,568.98		

Solution

Note that not all the cost codes are affected by the final week's purchases.

Look at each invoice in turn and be careful to identify correctly the code to be used for each cost.

Code	Year to date	Update	Closing balance at 30 September 20X7
	£	£	£
001001	254,867.00	23,500.00	278,367.00
001002	23,456.00	8,000.00	31,456.00
001003	15,345.00	4,500.00	19,845.00
002001	25,346.00	2,700.00	28,046.00
002002	7,345.00	3,000.00	10,345.00
002003	5,675.00		
006237	7,568.98	5,372.50	12,941.48

2.2 Ledger accounts

It is also possible that you may have to extract figures for materials costs, labour costs or expenses from ledger accounts in the cost accounting ledger records. Therefore you will need an outline understanding of how these figures are recorded in the cost accounting ledgers.

2.3 Materials accounting

When materials are purchased by the business they are recorded as a debit entry in the materials control account. When materials are issued to production, via a materials requisition, they are credited to the materials account and debited to the work in progress control account.

> ### :💡: Example
>
> During the month of May £100,000 of materials were purchased but only £90,000 of materials were issued to the production process.
>
> | | Materials controls account | | |
> |---|---|---|---|
> | | £ | | £ |
> | Purchases | 100,000 | Work in progress | 90,000 |
>
> | | Work in progress control account | | |
> |---|---|---|---|
> | | £ | | £ |
> | Purchases | 100,000 | Work in progress | 90,000 |
>
> Therefore if the amount of materials used for production in the month were required for comparison this could be found either by locating the debit entry in the work in progress control account or the credit entry in the materials control account.

2.4 Accounting for labour costs

As with the materials cost the production labour cost for the period will be entered as a debit entry in the work in progress control account. However this figures comes from the gross wages control which will initially record the total wages cost.

> ### :💡: Example
>
> The business incurs £60,000 of wages costs for the month of which £45,000 were paid to production staff and £15,000 to general administration staff.
>
> | | Gross wages control account | | |
> |---|---|---|---|
> | | £ | | £ |
> | Total gross wages | 60,000 | Work in progress | 45,000 |
> | | | Administration costs | 15,000 |
>
> | | Work in progress control account | | |
> |---|---|---|---|
> | | £ | | £ |
> | Materials control account | 90,000 | | |
> | Gross wages control | 45,000 | | |

The total wages from the gross wages control account are split between those relating to production which are debited to the work in progress account and those relating to other areas of the business, such as administration labour costs, are kept separate.

If the manufacturing labour cost for the month is required then this can be found either from the credit entry in the gross wages control account or the debit entry in the work in progress account.

2.5 Accounting for expenses

As with materials and labour costs, any expenses that are directly related to production are gathered together in the work in progress control account.

Example

The business incurs £10,000 of production expenses and £6,000 of administration expenses during the month.

	Expenses control account		
	£		£
Expenses incurred	16,000	Work in progress	10,000
		Administration expenses	6,000

	Work in progress control account		
	£		£
Materials control account	90,000		
Gross wages control	45,000		
Expenses control	10,000		

2.6 Comparisons

Now that we have determined how to gather both the historic and the current information it is now possible to consider how to make useful comparisons.

3 Previous periods, corresponding periods and forecasts

3.1 Comparison of information

There are many ways in which you might be requested to compare current costs and income to previous and corresponding control periods. In this section some typical examples will be considered.

It is always important to ensure that you understand precisely what is required of you as this comparison is likely to be a time consuming process and you do not want to waste time extracting information that is not required. Therefore if you have any doubts about precisely what information is required then always check with the appropriate person.

Example

Your organisation operates its sales function in three divisions, A, B and C and records sales separately for each division. You have been asked to compare this month's sales (June) to those of the previous month. You have found the May information from the management accounting filing system and they are as follows:

	£
Division A	113,000
Division B	258,000
Division C	142,000

You have also found the sales ledger accounts for June which are as follows:

Sales account – Division A

	£		£
		Sales June	129,000

Sales account – Division B

	£		£
Sales returns June	15,000	Sales June	250,000

Sales account – Division C

	£		£
		Sales June	120,000

You are required to compare the sales for June to those for the month of May in a suitable manner.

Probably the simplest method of comparing this information would be in the form of a table showing the sales for each division and in total for each month. Care should be taken with Division B's sales and the returns must be deducted from the sales figure therefore a net sales balance should be found on that account as follows:

Sales account – Division B

	£		£
Sales returns June	15,000	Sales June	250,000
Balance c/d	235,000		
	250,000		250,000

Now a simple table can be prepared

Divisional sales for May and June

	May	*June*	*Increase/ (decrease)*
	£	£	£
Division A	113,000	129,000	16,000
Division B	258,000	235,000	(23,000)
Division C	142,000	120,000	(22,000)
Total	513,000	484,000	(29,000)

It might also be useful to include a further column to show the percentage increase or decrease in sales. The percentage change would be calculated as a percentage of the May sales as follows:

Division A $\dfrac{16,000}{113,000} \times 100 = 14.2\%$

Division B $\dfrac{(23,000)}{258,000} \times 100 = (8.9\%)$

Division C $\dfrac{(22,000)}{142,000} \times 100 = (15.5\%)$

Total $\dfrac{(29,000)}{513,000} \times 100 = (5.7\%)$

The table would then appear as follows:

Divisional sales for May and June

	May	June	Increase/ (decrease)	Increase/ (decrease)
	£	£	£	%
Division A	113,000	129,000	16,000	14.2
Division B	258,000	235,000	(23,000)	(8.9)
Division C	142,000	120,000	(22,000)	(15.5)
Total	513,000	484,000	(29,000)	(5.7)

Activity 1

You have been asked to compare the month 2 labour cost from last year to the month 2 labour cost for this year.

From the filed management accounts for last year you discover that the month 2 labour cost was broken down as follows:

	£
Production labour cost	336,000
Selling department labour cost	248,000
Administration department labour cost	100,000

The wages expense account for month 2 of this year is as follows:

Wages expenses account

	£		£
Gross wages cost	990,000	Work-in-progress account	510,000
		Selling costs account	350,000
		Administration costs account	130,000

You are required to compare the labour costs for month 2 of the current period and the corresponding period.

3.2 Comparison to corresponding period

Rather than comparing figures from one month to the next or one quarter to the next it might be more useful to management to compare the figures for a particular period this year to the same period the previous year and determine any increases or decreases.

Example

In an earlier example we were given the total costs for the year to date as at 30 September for a variety of cost codes as follows:

Code	Year to date at 30 September 20X5
	£
021113	32,477
021114	146,229
021115	24,110
022113	66,001
022114	7,698
022115	13,332

The current year is 20X5 and you now find in the management accounting records the figures for the same cost codes in the year to date to 30 September 20X4. Comparison can then be made:

Code	Year to date at 30 September 20X4	Year to date at 30 September 20X5	Increase/ (decrease)
	£	£	£
021113	30,551	32,477	1,926
021114	151,345	146,229	(5,116)
021115	26,790	24,110	(1,680)
022113	73,465	66,001	(7,464)
022114	6,124	7,698	1,574
022115	11,531	13,332	1,801
	299,806	290,847	(8,959)

3.3 Comparison to budgeted figures

Comparison might also be required between forecast or budgeted figures for a period and the actual results of the period. Upon comparing actual costs to budgeted costs, there may be a difference or discrepancy between them, known as the variance. If the actual cost is greater than the budget, this is an adverse variance. If the actual cost is less than budget, this is a favourable variance.

Example

The budgeted costs for week 17 for material and labour production costs were found in the filing system and it was discovered that they were as follows:

	£
Material X	117,000
Material Y	270,000
Labour	226,000

The actual costs of the period are as follows:

Stores ledger card

MATERIAL DESCRIPTION Material X

Code M100

	Receipts			Issues			Balance		
Date	Quantity	Unit price £	Total £	Quantity	Unit price £	Total £	Quantity	Unit price £	Total £
Bal b/f							10,000	15.00	150,000
Week 17				8,000	15.00	120,000	2,000	15.00	30,000

MATERIAL DESCRIPTION Material Y

Code M101

	Receipts			Issues			Balance		
Date	Quantity	Unit price £	Total £	Quantity	Unit price £	Total £	Quantity	Unit price £	Total £
Bal b/f							130,000	2.50	325,000
Week 17				100,000	2.50	250,000	30,000	2.50	75,000

Wages expenses account

	£		£
Gross wages cost	470,000	Production costs	230,000
		Selling costs account	110,000
		Administration costs	130,000

You have been asked to prepare a comparison of the budgeted cost of materials and labour for production in week 17 to the actual cost for the week.

Solution

Costs – week 17

	Budget £	Actual £	Variance £
Material X	117,000	120,000	3,000 adverse
Material Y	270,000	250,000	20,000 favourable
Labour	226,000	230,000	4,000 adverse

Note how variances can be either favourable or adverse depending upon whether the actual cost is smaller or larger than the budget cost.

Activity 2

The budgeted costs for expected production of 100,000 units last week are given below:

	£
Labour	45,000
Materials	60,000
Production expenses	17,000

The actual costs were:

	£
Labour	42,000
Materials	62,000
Production expenses	16,000

You are required to compare budgeted costs to actual costs.

3.4 Sales and variances

Budgeted levels of sales can also be compared to actual sales and variances can be calculated. However some care should be taken with determining whether the sales variances are favourable or adverse. If actual sales are higher than budgeted sales then this is a favourable variance. Whereas, if actual sales are lower than the budgeted sales then this is an adverse variance.

:bulb: **Example**

Given below are the budgeted and actual sales for three products for the month of July and their variances. Make sure that you are happy with whether the variance is favourable or adverse.

Product	Budgeted sales £	Actual £	Variance £
X	450,000	430,000	20,000 adverse
Y	500,000	530,000	30,000 favourable
Z	410,000	400,000	10,000 adverse

:bulb: **Example**

XYZ Ltd has the following budget and actual results for August 20X6

	Budget August 20X6 £	Actual August 20X6 £
Sales	434,000	489,000
Costs		
Materials	178,000	193,000
Labour	50,000	56,000
Direct expenses	24,000	33,000
Indirect expenses	37,000	28,000
Total costs	289,000	310,000
Net profit	145,000	179,000

Compare budgeted and actual revenue, costs and profit, calculate the variances and state whether the variances are favourable or adverse.

Solution

	Budget August 20X6 £	Actual August 20X6 £	Variance £	
Sales	434,000	489,000	55,000	Fav
Costs				
Materials	178,000	193,000	15,000	Adv
Labour	50,000	56,000	6,000	Adv
Direct expenses	24,000	33,000	9,000	Adv
Indirect expenses	37,000	28,000	9,000	Fav
Total costs	289,000	310,000	21,000	Adv
Net profit	145,000	179,000	34,000	Fav

3.5 Investigation of variances

Variances are of interest to management as they form part of the management process of control and managers will often need to investigate the cause of any variances. However in many organisations not all variances will be investigated only those that are significant. Therefore you might be asked to prepare calculations showing each variance as a percentage of the budgeted figure indicating which are most significant and may deserve investigating.

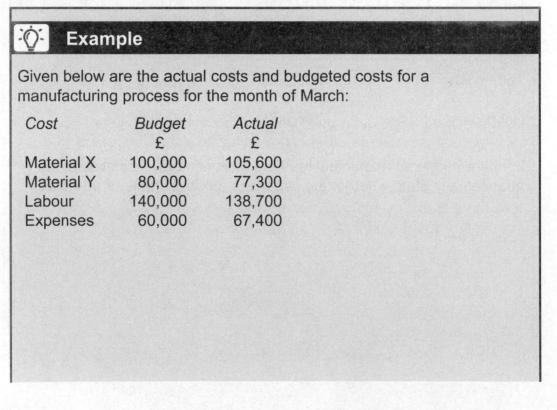

Example

Given below are the actual costs and budgeted costs for a manufacturing process for the month of March:

Cost	Budget £	Actual £
Material X	100,000	105,600
Material Y	80,000	77,300
Labour	140,000	138,700
Expenses	60,000	67,400

We can now calculate the variances for each expense together with the percentage that each variance is of the original budgeted figure.

Cost	Budget £	Actual £	Variance £	Percentage
Material X	100,000	105,600	5,600 adverse	5.6% adverse
Material Y	80,000	77,300	2,700 favourable	3.4% favourable
Labour	140,000	138,700	1,300 favourable	0.9% favourable
Expenses	60,000	67,400	7,400 adverse	12.3% adverse

If the business has a policy of only investigating variances that are more than 10% of the budgeted figure then in this case only the expenses variance needs to be highlighted for investigation to management.

Example

Consider again the information for XYZ Ltd

	Budget August 20X6 £	Actual August 20X6 £
Sales	434,000	489,000
Costs		
Materials	178,000	193,000
Labour	50,000	56,000
Direct expenses	24,000	33,000
Indirect expenses	37,000	28,000
Total costs	289,000	310,000
Net profit	145,000	179,000

Compare the budget and actual revenue and individual costs and calculate the percentage difference for each as a percentage of the budget figure. Calculate the variance to two decimal places.

XYZ Ltd has a policy of investigating any variances that are more than 10% of budget. Which variances would they investigate?

Solution

	Budget August 20X6 £	Actual August 20X6 £	Variance £	Percentage difference %
Sales	434,000	489,000	55,000	12.67
Costs				
Materials	178,000	193,000	15,000	8.43
Labour	50,000	56,000	6,000	12.00
Direct expenses	24,000	33,000	9,000	37.50
Indirect expenses	37,000	28,000	9,000	23.32
Total costs	289,000	310,000		
Net profit	145,000	179,000		

XYZ Ltd would investigate all the variances except materials.

4 Confidentiality

4.1 Introduction

As part of the accounting team you will often find that you have access to documents and information about the organisation that other employees do not have. It is extremely important that you are always discreet and strictly follow all the confidentiality guidelines of your organisation.

4.2 Sales information

When dealing with sales invoices and credit customers it is likely that you may come across information regarding customers' credit ratings and financial position. Such information should never be disclosed.

4.3 Materials and expenses

When dealing with materials costs and expense details there may be many confidential areas that you come across, from suppliers' details to sales representatives' expense claims.

4.4 Labour costs

Perhaps most importantly, when dealing with labour costs you may become aware of many personal details about employees within the organisation. Such information should always be treated with the greatest degree of confidentiality.

5 Methods of reporting

When a request is made for such a comparison of information it will normally be requested in a particular format. This can range from an informal note through to a formal report. In this chapter we will consider each of the different methods of reporting.

5.1 House style

Although the basic requirements of each method of reporting will be covered in this chapter it is important to realise that each organisation will have its own style and methods of reporting. These will normally be contained in the organisation's policy manual and house styles should always be followed.

5.2 Confidentiality

It is extremely important that the information that has been requested is sent to the appropriate person and only that person and any others that you are specifically asked to send it to. Often the information is confidential and therefore should be treated with the highest respect and care.

6 A note

Probably the most simple and informal method of reporting information to another person in the organisation is by way of a note.

6.1 Format

There is no set format for a note although obviously it must be addressed to the appropriate person, be dated, be headed up correctly so that the recipient knows what it is about and include your name so that the recipient knows who it is from.

In most cases the information that you are reporting on will be important management information and therefore it is unlikely that a note would usually be the most appropriate format. Only use a note if specifically asked to by the person requesting the information.

7 A letter

A slightly more formal method of communicating information is in the form of a letter. However it would be quite unusual to communicate to another person in the same organisation in this way. A letter however may be appropriate if the person to whom you are sending the information works in a separate location.

7.1 Format

A letter should always have a letter heading showing the organisation's name, address, telephone number etc. Most organisations will have pre-printed letterheads for you to use.

The letter must also be dated and the name and address of the recipient be included before the letter itself is started.

The method of signing a letter will depend upon the formality of the how the letter begins.

If a letter is started as 'Dear Sir' then the appropriate way to sign off the letter is 'Yours faithfully'.

However if the letter is started 'Dear Mr Smith' then the appropriate way to sign off the letter is 'Yours sincerely'.

8 Electronic mail

Most organisations are now fully computerised and most individuals within an organisation can communicate with each other via electronic mail or email

8.1 Format

An email must be addressed to the person to whom it is being sent using their email address. It should also be given a title so that the recipient can see at a glance who it is from and what it is about.

In terms of format of the content of the email there are no rules other than any organisational procedures that should be followed.

Always spell check your emails before sending them!

9 Memoranda

Definition

A memorandum (or memo) is a written communication between two persons within an organisation. The plural of memorandum is memoranda.

A memorandum serves a similar purpose to a letter. However the main difference is that letters are usually sent to persons outside the organisation, whereas memoranda or memos are for communication within the organisation itself. Memos can range from brief handwritten notes, to typed sets of instructions to a junior, to a more formal report to a superior. In general a memo can be used for any purpose where written communication is necessary within the organisation, provided this is according to the rules of the organisation.

Planning and organising work 5

Introduction

Planning at the organisational level is the process of deciding what should be done, who should do it and when and how it should be done. At the individual level it involves scheduling routine tasks so that they will be completed in time and working into the routine any urgent tasks that interrupt the usual level of working. Work planning means establishing priorities and allocating and scheduling tasks using planning aids such as lists, action plans, timetables, diaries and charts.

KNOWLEDGE	CONTENTS
3.1 Plan and manage your own workload effectively and prioritise tasks.	1 Organisational objectives
	2 Organisation structure
	3 Work planning
	4 Planning methods
	5 Time management
	6 Difficulties in meeting deadlines

1 Organisational objectives

1.1 Introduction

An organisation will establish goals, objectives and strategies and then determine the policies and procedures necessary to achieve its stated aims. Its effectiveness is generally determined by how well the objectives are being achieved.

Once the objectives are set management will structure the tasks that need to be performed, and decide which department and which individuals will complete which task and when.

1.2 Work methods and practices

The work methods and practices are influenced by:

- the job that needs to be done – its purpose, manner, order and deadline

- the law – making sure the job is done in a safe and secure manner in accordance with the regulations and codes of practice

- the culture of the organisation – the 'way we do things round here' based on the organisation and work group's values.

The work methods chosen should bring together the above to ensure jobs gets done in the right order and in the best way possible in accordance with legal requirements and the organisation's procedures. There should be no duplication or part cover of the work and efforts should be harnessed to a common goal.

1.3 Performance and motivation

Recognising appropriate direction techniques requires identification and selection of the most efficient means of stimulating outstanding performance.

The work methods and practices chosen by the organisation will not work to get the job done unless the person chosen to do the job is sufficiently able and motivated.

One of the models of motivation shows what job performance depends on:

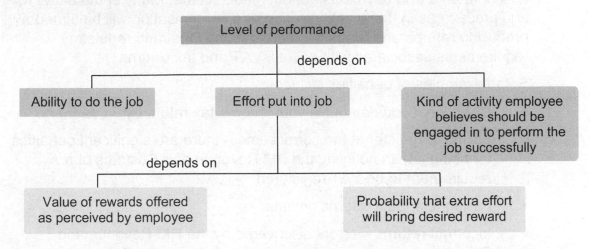

This model shows that in any given situation the greater the number and variety of rewards available to an employee, the greater is the probability that extra effort will be put into attaining the targets set, in the hope of gaining the rewards desired.

1.4   Legal, regulatory and organisational requirements

Laws or agreements of confidentiality will cover some information from within your organisation. For example, you may be required by contract not to disclose financial information. Many of the activities and procedures in the finance section of an organisation will be aimed at producing returns and forms to conform to the legal and regulatory requirements associated with payroll, VAT and tax returns.

The legal and regulatory requirements that you must consider are those under the Data Protection Act and the Companies Act.

The Data Protection Act – is all about protecting data concerning individuals where this data is processed automatically i.e., by computer. This is important from your work point of view in that personal details of employees are confidential under the Act and you might have access to these if you are dealing with payroll details. Because computers can bring together vast amounts of information, process it rapidly and transfer it instantly anywhere in the world, there is an inherent danger that information could be corrupted, used out of context or lost in the system, with the result that individuals would suffer.

The Companies Act – provides a statutory framework for the preparation of the accounts of limited companies. It outlines formats, fundamental accounting principles, valuation rules and possible exemptions for small and medium-sized companies.

The most important deadlines for a company are those where penalties arise if returns and payments are not made in time. Many of the activities and procedures in the finance section of an organisation will be aimed at producing returns and forms to conform to the legal and regulatory requirements associated with payroll, VAT and tax returns.

Some examples of penalties include:

*   £100 fine if you do not file your income tax return by 31 January.

*   Failing to register at the correct time – there are significant penalties for being late in notifying the HM Revenue and Customs of a requirement to be VAT registered.

*   Failing to submit returns on time.

*   Incorrect returns – errors discovered by the HM Revenue and Customs may carry a 15% misdeclaration penalty. Failure to submit an EU sales statement may give rise to penalties.

*   Record-keeping – you need to record all your business transactions, and keep documents including bank statements, bills, receipts and cheque stubs to back them up. You also need to separate your business transactions from your personal finances.

Rather like keeping records for HM Revenue and Customs, you need to be meticulous about VAT. For VAT purposes, you must keep a record of all the supplies you make and receive, and a summary of VAT for each tax period covered by your tax returns. Records must be up to date and easy to find, and if you register for VAT you must keep your records for six years.

2   Organisation structure

2.1   Structural relationships

There are different ways of looking at this topic. We can start with the structural types of roles and relationships that show how power, authority and influence are built into the organisation. Working relationships can also be considered in terms of their contractual, ethical and legal effect. Overlaid on the structural factors, there are interpersonal relationships, which include team working, interdepartmental relations and networking.

The formal structure, communications and procedures of the organisation are based on authority, responsibility and functional relationships. You need to know what areas you have authority over and how far that authority extends – who you report to and who reports to you. The basic relationship in an organisation is that between superior and subordinate. The superior has authority i.e. the right or power to make decisions or give instructions or orders to the subordinate.

There are also the peer relationships – people you work with and who share similar goals to you. Your plans and schedules need to dovetail with those of other individuals and teams with whom your work is linked.

In most organisations this role and the responsibilities involved in the role will be determined by the job description. Every employee should have a detailed job description. Only then can one fully appreciate one's own role and responsibilities.

As well as being aware of your role and responsibilities, in some organisations there is a process of management by objectives (MBO) in which your supervisor or manager will agree specific, measurable goals with you on a regular basis. He or she will also agree on working methods and schedules as well as agree the resources to complete the job. You are then responsible for attaining these goals within a certain time. After this time has elapsed you should meet up with your superior again to discuss results and establish new objectives.

2.2   Authority and responsibility

Organisation structure is the division of work among members of the organisation and the co-ordination of their activities so they are directed towards the goals and objectives of the organisation. It means grouping people into departments or sections, defining tasks and responsibilities, work roles and relationships and channels of communication and allocating authority and responsibility.

Q Definition

Authority can be defined as the right that an individual has to require certain actions of others i.e. it is the right to use power.

Responsibility is the duty of an official to carry out his or her assigned task or to get others to do it.

Delegation is the act by which a person transfers part of their authority to a subordinate person.

This creates a hierarchy or chain of command where authority flows downwards from the top management to each level of the organisation. This chain is illustrated on the next page with the arrows down showing the delegation:

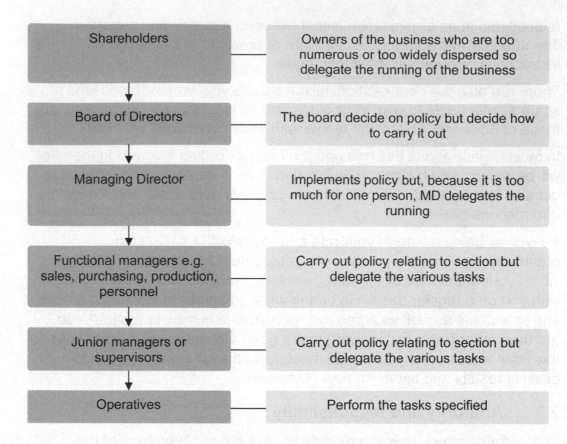

The chain of delegation gives employees the means to resolve or refer any problems or queries regarding work activities to the appropriate person.

2.3 Organisational and departmental structure

An organisation must be set up in a formal manner to give it some authority or some standing. This means that those within the organisation must be organised so that they know what to do and whom to ask for advice.

* An organisation chart describes in diagrammatic form the structure of the organisation. It illustrates who communicates with whom, how the control system works, who is in control, who has authority and above all, who is responsible. It shows:

    – direction of responsibility (the chart indicates the direct relationship between a group and its immediate supervisor and subordinates)

    – relationships between various sections within a department.

It can outline areas of responsibility for each department and line manager and be extended down to individual employees if necessary.

There are a number of ways to show the grouping of people in the organisation. The functional structure (see below) shows responsibility allocated to specialised functions:

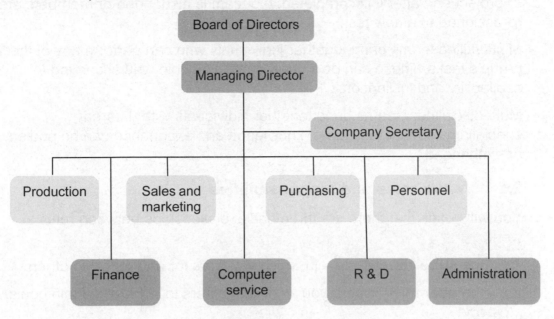

The organisation chart of the finance department might be shown as:

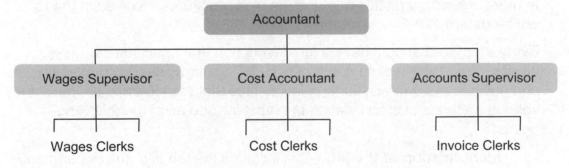

2.4   Teams and teamwork

The basic work unit of organisations has traditionally been the functional department, such as accounting or sales. In more recent times, organisations have adopted smaller, more flexible and responsible units – set up as matrix structures, which tend to favour team working.. This allows work to be shared among a number of individuals so that it gets done more efficiently and effectively than by individuals working alone. Teams are particularly effective for increasing communication, generating new ideas and evaluating ideas from different viewpoints.

A team may be set up as a separate unit on a more or less permanent basis, with responsibilities for a certain product or stage of a process; alternatively, it may be on a temporary basis for the attainment of the task or project and after it is completed, the team is disbanded or members are re-assigned to a new task.

Multi-skilled teams bring together individuals who can perform any of the group's tasks. These can be shared out in a flexible way according to availability and inclination.

Multi-disciplinary teams bring together individuals with different specialisms so that their skills, knowledge and experience can be pooled or exchanged.

2.5 Work roles and responsibilities

You will notice that there are three basic relationships between roles at work:

1   the **subordinate** role – in which you work for and report to others

2   the **peer** role – where you work with others to achieve certain goals, and

3   the **authority** role – where other people work for and report to you.

In most organisations this role and the responsibilities involved in the role will be determined by the job description.

Every employee should have a job description that specifies the tasks; details responsibilities; sets authority limits; distinguishes accountability; and outlines the organisational relationships that the job entails. There are various methods of classification but most include all of the following points:

- **Identification of the job** – this includes the job title, the department/ organisation structure and the number of people doing the job.

- **Purpose of the job** – identifying its objectives in relationship to overall objectives, e.g. to manage the manufacturing unit of the department making garden gnomes and plant pots.

- **Position in the organisation** indicating the relationships with other jobs and the chains of responsibility. For this purpose, many firms refer to existing organisation charts.

- **Duties** – the principal duties to be performed, with emphasis on key tasks, and limits to the job-holder's authority. Usually under this heading is included an indication of how the job differs from others in the organisation. A further breakdown of principal duties is made identifying specific tasks in terms of what precisely is done and in what manner, and with some explanation, both in terms of quantity and quality. When listing all the tasks involved it is preferable to use an active verb to precede each duty e.g. types letters to clients; lists totals of debtors.

- **Responsibilities** – a statement outlining the responsibilities for the resources e.g. staff, money and machinery.

- **Physical conditions** – including details of noisy, dirty, dangerous conditions or pleasant office conditions, and also hours of work, overtime, unsocial hours etc.

- **Social conditions** – the type of group the employee will be concerned with.

- **Grade and salary/wage range and fringe benefits** – details of the rates for the grade, increments, piece-work, bonuses and commission, plus fringe benefits such as luncheon vouchers, pension schemes, company car, etc.

- **Promotion prospects** – to whom the job reports and at what level, with possible indications about future succession, prospects of promotion or transfer.

- **Key difficulties** – no job description is complete without a full identification of the key difficulties likely to be encountered by the job-holder.

You should try to ensure that you have a detailed job description. Only then can you fully appreciate your own role and responsibilities.

For example you are a sales ledger clerk with certain responsibilities for a number of customer accounts. You have made an appointment with the sales ledger manager to discuss the credit limits of seven of your current customers. During the course of the meeting with your manager he makes it quite clear that the subject of credit limits is the sole responsibility of another member of the staff. They are quite clearly outside of your own responsibilities.

The result of not knowing your own role and responsibilities has meant wasted time for both yourself and your manager.

2.6 Colleagues' work roles and responsibilities

If you wish to discuss a work related matter then an initial problem is who is the appropriate or relevant member of staff to discuss this matter with. This will usually depend on the roles and responsibilities of other members of staff, which you may not know in detail. However the options are usually as follows:

- **Line managers** – these are managers who manage various areas or departments of a business, for example the production manager, sales manager, marketing manager, finance manager etc. If the matter to be discussed appears to be important or personal then the appropriate line manager will probably be the person to approach.

- **Immediate colleagues** – if the matter to be discussed is regarding, perhaps, advice as to how to approach a routine task then a colleague with more experience than yourself might be the appropriate person. It is worth bearing in mind that a great deal can be learnt from colleagues with greater experience than oneself.

- **Other members of staff with related work activities** – in many instances knowledge and understanding of a particular matter will be shared by a number of members of staff throughout the organisation, even though they are in different departments or activity areas. These could be the appropriate people to discuss matters with in certain circumstances.

In practice, it may be difficult to know exactly who is the appropriate member of staff for a particular piece of information or message. It is unlikely that each individual fully understands the role and responsibilities of all other individuals in the organisation.

You should be aware of the line and staff relations in your organisational structure. Draw an organisation chart of your company, putting names and a brief job description beside the line managers, immediate colleagues and other members of staff with related work activities.

Knowing who does what and where, enables you to:

- communicate more freely and efficiently

- seek and exchange information, advice and support

- negotiate the assistance of others

- transfer telephone calls to the right person

- deliver mail accurately

- handle any enquiries effectively.

3 Work planning

3.1 Planning and organising

All levels of management are involved in planning. At the top level decisions are made on what to do and as you come down the hierarchy the plan is fleshed out to incorporate how it is to be done and when it is going to be done.

Organising is the next stage after planning. It means working out the actual jobs needed to be done to fulfil the plans agreed upon, grouping activities into a pattern or structure and giving specific jobs to people in the organisation to achieve the plans agreed upon and setting deadlines for their completion.

At the individual level work planning involves scheduling and timetabling routine tasks so that they will be completed at the right time and handling high priority tasks and deadlines, which interrupt the usual level of working.

The basic steps and objectives in work planning include the following:

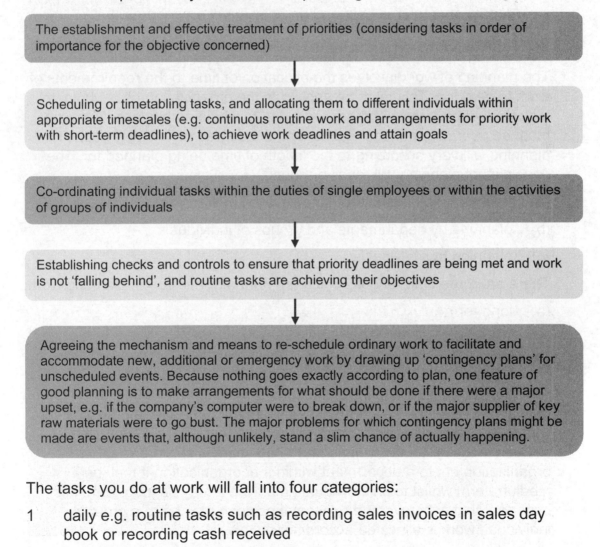

The establishment and effective treatment of priorities (considering tasks in order of importance for the objective concerned)

Scheduling or timetabling tasks, and allocating them to different individuals within appropriate timescales (e.g. continuous routine work and arrangements for priority work with short-term deadlines), to achieve work deadlines and attain goals

Co-ordinating individual tasks within the duties of single employees or within the activities of groups of individuals

Establishing checks and controls to ensure that priority deadlines are being met and work is not 'falling behind', and routine tasks are achieving their objectives

Agreeing the mechanism and means to re-schedule ordinary work to facilitate and accommodate new, additional or emergency work by drawing up 'contingency plans' for unscheduled events. Because nothing goes exactly according to plan, one feature of good planning is to make arrangements for what should be done if there were a major upset, e.g. if the company's computer were to break down, or if the major supplier of key raw materials were to go bust. The major problems for which contingency plans might be made are events that, although unlikely, stand a slim chance of actually happening.

The tasks you do at work will fall into four categories:

1   daily e.g. routine tasks such as recording sales invoices in sales day book or recording cash received

2   weekly e.g. preparing journal entries to post totals from books of prime entry to nominal ledger

3   monthly e.g. bank reconciliation or sales ledger reconciliation

4   one-off e.g. information for a report.

Most employees in an organisation will spend the majority of their time working on the routine tasks that are part of their job and responsibilities. However at times unexpected and non-routine tasks may arise. These must also be dealt with without affecting the routine responsibilities. The performance criterion states that you should:

- identify and prioritise tasks according to organisational procedures and regulatory requirements

- recognise changes in priorities and adapt resources allocations and work plans accordingly

- check that work methods and activities conform to legal and regulatory requirements and organisational procedures.

3.2 Agreeing timescales

The planning of work involves the allocation of time to the requirements of work to be done. This must be applied to the organisation as a whole, to individual departments and sections, and to single employees. Planning must be geared to periods of time, and the degree of flexibility built into planning will vary according to the length of time being planned for. The principles of planning will revolve around:

(a) determining the length of time covered by the plans

(b) planning by departments and groups of individuals

(c) planning by individuals.

There are three time ranges, which are normally involved in planning work:

(a) long-term

(b) medium-term

(c) short-term.

These three terms are really only expressions of convenience. Time is relative. For example, a length of five years might be considered long-term within an organisation producing footwear but short-term in, say, the aviation industry. It may well be that three years is short-term to an organisation but to a department within that organisation it may be medium-term whilst to an individual employee it may be long-term. It is important that, whatever the relevant time span may be to a group or individual, work is allocated accordingly.

3.3 Identifying priorities

Much office work is of a routine nature although there are exceptions. Priorities must be established with regard to the cyclical nature of routine work and unexpected demands.

The cyclical nature of routine work often means that certain tasks have to be completed by a certain time. In such cases other work may have to be left in order to ensure that the task with the approaching deadline date is given priority. Such tasks might include:

- the preparation of payroll sheets for a weekly computer run

- the despatch of monthly statements to account customers

- the checking of stock levels at predetermined intervals and appropriate action such as re-ordering.

Unexpected demands are often made at departmental, sectional or individual level. If management requires urgent or additional work to be carried out then, obviously, some other tasks will have to be postponed.

Given that routine tasks may be anticipated and that unexpected demands cannot, this area of priority identification can be divided into routine tasks, which can be accommodated within normal sensible planning and 'emergency-type' tasks that must be performed at short notice.

Routine work usually includes a number of tasks that, as a matter of course, fall into a natural order in which they should be performed. This 'natural order of events' approach can usually be incorporated into the normal routine of the

office and/or the individual to such an extent that often it is not apparent that there has ever been a problem with the identification of priority tasks.

Where tasks/events of an 'emergency-type' nature arise the main problem facing an individual will be that of deciding which of the routine tasks should be postponed. However, the postponement of one routine task will automatically delay successive tasks.

3.4 Guidelines for determining priorities

In determining priorities, the following should be noted.

- Wherever it is possible for a priority to be anticipated, such as in the case of the 'natural order of events' described above, then associated difficulties will usually be overcome by sensible, logical planning.

- If an 'emergency type' task occurs, then normal routine work will automatically take second place. It is here that decisions must be taken to decide which routine tasks should be postponed. Also, plans should be formulated and implemented to ensure that the routine work postponed is carried out as soon as possible, resulting in minimum disruption to the normal routine.

Often there may arise situations where one priority comes into conflict with another. Here the task deemed more important by a responsible individual should take preference.

Unfortunately, individuals within one department or section often become blind to the needs of other departments or sections. A task that is classed as low priority within one department or section may be of the utmost priority to another. Thus in arriving at any decision the individual making that decision must ensure that the effect on each department is included in the decision-making process.

A responsible individual should determine priorities. Often, especially in the matter of routine cycles, the individual responsible for that work will be qualified to determine any priority. However, the greater the effect and the wider the span of influence of priority determination, the more responsible the individual should be.

When an unexpected task is given to you then you must have the flexibility to be able to reschedule your routine work in order to complete this task.

3.5 Setting priorities

Activities need to be sequenced and scheduled. There may be conflict between the two planning tasks since the best sequence of activities to put the plan into place might not be consistent with the schedule of when particular activities need to be completed. The sequence of activities may be determined by the following:

- An activity must precede another when it is a pre-requisite for later activities. Assembly of a car cannot precede the manufacture or purchase of its components.

- The sequence of activities may be dictated by the ease with which they can be done. New products or services are often introduced into the most receptive parts of the market first.

- An activity may be considered more important than others, e.g. in the building industry priority will be given to outdoor work when the weather is favourable to minimise the risk of delays later.

The organisation's operations require proper scheduling of resources to run efficiently and avoid periods of over and under utilisation. Some activities must occur at precisely the right time, e.g. specific day and time slot for advertising a new product. The scheduling of tasks can also affect customer service in terms of delivery.

3.6 Prioritisation of routine tasks

Routine tasks may be tasks that are performed a number of times each day, tasks performed once or twice each day, tasks necessary each week, or at the end of each month perhaps.

Examples of routine tasks might include the following:

- sending out of invoices to customers each day
- opening the post at the beginning of the day and again after the second post has arrived
- filing all copy invoices at the end of the week
- preparing a list of outstanding customer balances at the end of each month.

Priorities are tasks listed in order of importance. Each day employees will need to prioritise the tasks that they are required to do during that day.

The first job of the day might be to open the post, as the post may contain urgent items to be dealt with by yourself or other members of the department. This will therefore be a high priority job and should not be left until the middle of the morning.

If your job includes responsibility for sending out invoices to customers then it will be a fairly high priority that these invoices are sent out on the same day as the sale or customer order. The task of filing copies of the invoices is less urgent. It may be possible to leave this until later in the day, or even later in the week.

Another skill you can use to analyse jobs is sequencing. When you put things in sequence, you arrange steps in the order that you do them. When you work out the sequence to carry out the tasks, you are judging two things:

- How urgent is the task?
- How important is the task?

These are not the same thing. Urgent tasks need to be completed within a particular time limit. Important jobs may affect a lot of people or cost a lot of money. They may also have major implications if they are not done, or if they are done badly. If you are going abroad on holiday, it is important that you have a passport. If your holiday isn't for six months, it isn't urgent. It becomes urgent if you leave it too late.

3.7 Prioritisation of unexpected tasks

Unexpected or non-routine tasks will normally occur for one of two reasons.

1   The unexpected tasks may be due to additional activity in the organisation, such as a new product launch or takeover of another company.

2   Unexpected tasks can also occur due to some 'emergency' within the organisation such as a fellow member of staff being off work sick or an error being found which must be dealt with immediately.

They should be fairly easy to identify, as they will normally involve instruction from a more senior member of staff. For example if a member of your department is off sick, and is unlikely to return for the rest of the week, it is likely that the manager or supervisor will re-schedule that person's tasks to be dealt with by the other members of the department.

However some unexpected tasks might not be so clearly signalled. For example suppose that you answer the telephone for a colleague during his lunch break.

The call is from a customer with an urgent request for information then this customer query may be an unexpected task that you will need to deal with.

If an unexpected task is identified then this must also be prioritised and fitted in with the routine tasks of the individual's job. Unexpected tasks will not always be necessarily urgent, although many will be. When an unexpected task is identified the individual should ensure that he or she fully understands the following points:

- the precise nature of the task

- the resources or information required to carry out the task

- the time required to obtain those resources or information

- the time that the task is expected to take (remember that as an unexpected task it is unlikely that the individual will have performed this task before)

- the time allowed for this task and deadline set for it

- the importance of the task

- the priority it should be allocated in respect of the work being carried out.

Only when aware of all of these points is it possible to correctly prioritise the task and schedule it together with their remaining routine tasks.

For example suppose that you are required to produce a report for a board meeting on Wednesday 12 March. Today is Monday 3 March. In order to produce the report you will require a number of files from the central filing system which are likely to take two days to be accessed and delivered. The manager of the department who has commissioned this report estimates that there will be approximately one full day's work obtaining the relevant information from the files and another half day in actually preparing the report itself. Owing to backlogs in the typing department your manager suggests that the report is with the typist by next Monday morning, 10 March, at the latest in order that it can be typed, proof read and any adjustments made in time for the board meeting on Wednesday 12 March.

In this instance the only task that you will need to perform immediately, a high priority today, is to inform central filing of the files that are required for the report. As the files will not reach you until Wednesday then there can be nothing else done for this task until that day. You must then ensure that during Wednesday, Thursday and Friday approximately a day and a half is set aside to prepare and write the report. You must also ensure that when the report is returned from typing at the beginning of the following week the proof reading is again given a high priority.

As a further example suppose that a colleague in your department has called in sick with flu this Monday morning. Your manager estimates that your colleague will not return to work this week and therefore all of his responsibilities must be dealt with by the other members of the department for the entire week. One of your colleague's responsibilities, which your manager has allocated to you, is to deal with customer complaints. It is the organisation's procedure to ensure that all complaints are dealt with, even if this is simply an acknowledging letter, on the same day as the complaint is received. Therefore, in order to comply with organisational procedures, you will need to give priority to any complaints received in the post each morning and any telephone complaints received during each day. Again you must also ensure that your own priority routine tasks, such as sending out invoices on the day of the order, are completed at the appropriate time.

Activity 1

List all of your routine daily tasks.

Make a separate list of all non-routine tasks that may arise, and state why they arise. (By their nature non-routine tasks are unexpected and you may need to invent possible non-routine tasks!)

3.8 Prioritisation using the Time Management Grid

Prioritisation is a difficult skill that many employees simply never learn to do – they never learn to distinguish between important and urgent. Something may be important (e.g. a report to management) but may not be urgent, it may not be required until next month. Something else may be urgent (requisition of copier paper which has run out) but it is not important!

What often tends to happen is that we do the easy or quick jobs first regardless of their urgency or importance. The trouble is that a lot of quick and easy jobs often take up an inordinate amount of time and have a habit of multiplying. Meanwhile important jobs that require a little more thought and effort are only forced upon us as they grow in urgency and deadlines approach. The longer an important job is kept waiting in the in-tray the more difficult it seems to grow in our minds! A further problem is that an important job done under time pressure is often not done as well as it could have been done given plenty of time. How often have we all wished we had started a difficult job much sooner!

Sometimes it helps to use the idea of importance and urgency to work out the order in which to do tasks. This diagram can help you to sort your tasks and plan when to do them.

	Urgent	**Not urgent**
Important	Must be done soon Do you need help?	Plan a time for it to be done
Unimportant	Can someone else do it? If not, do it quickly.	Does it need doing? Can someone else do it?

🔍 Definition

The **Time Management Grid** is a system of ranking jobs according to their urgency and their importance (with 1 being low and 10 being high). A grid is then drawn with important 1 to 10 on the y axis and urgent 1 to 10 on the x axis. The x and y axis intersect each other at 5. This creates four areas in the grid: Urgent and important; urgent but not important; important but not urgent; and finally, neither important nor urgent. From a list of jobs each one is given a ranking for urgency and importance, which can then be 'plotted' on the grid. This gives a graphical representation of how jobs should be prioritised.

The solution to the following activity demonstrates how a Time Management Grid should be drawn

📝 Activity 2

Write down a list of at least 8 to 10 jobs that you must do. Try to categorise them as important or urgent and rank them on a scale of 1 to 10 (with 10 being least important or urgent). Now look at the grid given in the answer, which shows how prioritisation can be illustrated graphically.

3.9   Change in priorities

The paragraphs so far have discussed the fact that if unexpected tasks are identified then the priorities of an individual may change. One of the performance criterion for this chapter states that 'where priorities change, work plans are changed accordingly'. If the priorities for a particular day change then it is highly likely that the work schedule must also be changed or adapted. For example suppose that an individual's schedule for a day showed the following tasks:

- open the post and deal with any urgent matters

- send out invoices for that day's orders

- fill out time sheet due in three day's time

- prepare notes for meeting with manager in one week's time.

When opening the post an urgent matter is discovered that is likely to take up to three hours of your time. Your manager is insistent that this matter must be dealt with today. In this case, unless you are to work for two or three extra hours in the day, the daily schedule will need adapting. The routine tasks that must be carried out each day must still also be done. Therefore the sending out of sales invoices must also take place in the day. However the filling out of the time sheet has three days of slack built into it and the preparation of notes for a meeting has a week of slack. Therefore these items can be viewed as far less urgent and may well be postponed to a later day.

When re-scheduling work for a day students should always ensure that items that must be done that day are covered. Only items with a degree of slack built into them i.e. items due at some point in the future can be postponed. When adapting or altering work schedules students should always bear in mind any effect that this will have on other members of staff and their own priorities and work schedules.

4   Planning methods

4.1   Introduction

Different organisations, groups and individuals have individual characteristics, tastes, styles, preferences and objectives. These particular objectives may well be attained via different methods and systems of scheduling work. As a method of planning group work, it is vital that these efforts are co-ordinated – not only with each other but with all actions taken. The method used can be a means of communication and support within the group, assuring all members of the group progress towards their goal.

The following planning methods and systems are probably the most common:

(a)   checklists

(b)   bar charts

(c)   bring-forward, bring-up and follow-up systems

(d)   activity scheduling and time scheduling

(e)   action sheets

(f)   other systems, including planning charts and boards, and diaries.

Each of these methods and systems will be discussed individually below. However, any combination may be in use at any one time within an organisation or by an individual employee. It is vital therefore that these efforts are co-ordinated, not only with each other but with all actions taken.

4.2   Checklists

Checklists are often used on an individual basis and are perhaps the simplest system, being essentially a list of items or activities. The preparation of a typical checklist would involve the following:

(a)   the formulation of a list of activities and tasks to be performed within a given period

(b)   the identification of urgent or priority tasks

(c)   the maintenance of a continuous checklist with the addition of extra activities and tasks as and when required.

This system is obviously limited in its application because of its simplicity. It is suited to fairly mundane or routine tasks, but it is these tasks, which are often the very essence of the attainment of objectives.

Typical uses of checklists would include the following:

(a)   purchasing requirements

(b)   points to cover at an interview

(c)   points to cover at a meeting (e.g. an agenda)

(d)   organising a conference or meeting.

Below is a checklist to show when certain returns associated with PAYE are due.

STATUTORY RETURNS SCHEDULE

Returns	Description	Date Due	Forward To
P60	This is a total of the employee's year-end earnings including tax and NI.	05.2006	Employee
P9D	Must be completed for all employees earning less than £8,500 (including reimbursed expenses and the taxable values of benefits) and for Directors for whom forms P11D are not required.	07.2006	Employee and HM Revenue and Customs
P14	Summary of deductions such as tax, NI, SSP, SMP.	05.2006	HM Revenue and Customs
P35	Statement of tax, NI, SSP and SMP for each employee together with an overall summary of the NI monthly or quarterly payments made by the employer in respect of that tax year	05.2006	HM Revenue and Customs
P38S	Relates to students who work for an employer during their holidays.	05.2006	HM Revenue and Customs
WTC	Year-end summary of Working Tax Credits paid to employees throughout the year.	05.2006	HM Revenue and Customs
DPTC	Year-end summary of Disabled Person's Tax Credit paid to employees throughout the year.	05.2006	HM Revenue and Customs

4.3   Bar charts

A bar chart has two main purposes:

(a)   to show the time necessary for an activity

(b)   to display the time relationship between one activity and another.

Bar charts are particularly useful for checking the time schedules for a number of activities that are interdependent. A bar chart for the building of a house extension might be shown over a period of six months and an example is given below.

Task	March	April	May	June	July	August
Dig foundations	▬					
Walls/floors		▬				
Windows			▬			
Door frames				▬		
Roof				▬		
Electric wiring				▬		
Plumbing			▬			
Glazing					▬	
Plastering						▬

This illustrates the importance of bar charts in showing:

(a)   overall progress to date, thus assisting in monitoring

(b)   the progress attained at an individual stage of a multi-stage process.

4.4   Bring-forward, bring-up and follow-up systems

These systems are more sophisticated than checklists and bar charts. They are particularly useful for coping with documentation and are utilised in many offices. The systems involve the filing of details of work to be done and the dates on which this work is to be done. A routine is established with a view to allocating necessary tasks to the precise day.

The systems all operate around the following principles:

A note is made of anything to be done in the future, showing details of the appropriate action or format (e.g. make a telephone call or write a letter)

The note is filed away in a concertina folder with separate files for each day

Each appropriate file is checked at the start of each day and the action required that day noted

The action is carried out

4.5 Activity scheduling

> ### Definition
>
> **Activity scheduling** is concerned with the determination of priority and the establishment of the order in which tasks are to be tackled. The establishment of an order of priority is not as easy in practice as it may appear in theory.

Some tasks must be completed before others may be commenced, some may need to be carried out at the same time as others and some may need to be completed at the same time as others but factors such as finance or manpower may prevent this. A typical problem that is particularly suited to activity scheduling is the arrangement of an interview where, say, three panel members are required and six candidates have been short-listed for interview. Obviously, mutually convenient dates must be found when all nine parties are available and the room, which is to be used for the interview, must be free for use on these days.

Activity scheduling involves the identification of key factors and their assembly on a checklist. In the example given above, the two key factors are room availability and people availability. It may be used for any task, which involves a number of actions that must necessarily be undertaken in some sequence.

4.6 Time scheduling

> ### Definition
>
> **Time scheduling** is an extension of activity scheduling by indicating the required time for each task. It follows the preparation of an activity schedule and involves the determination of time required for each activity.

Given that within an activity schedule some tasks will be performed simultaneously, it should be noted that the time period in which the series of activities will be completed may not equate to the total of the individual activity times.

Effectively a time schedule determines the order in which activities are scheduled on a checklist, the time required for each activity also being shown alongside each item. Tasks that can be done in parallel are noted. The total of the individual activity times, with allowances for simultaneous activities, will produce the time allowed for one complete group of activities.

Time scheduling is thus particularly useful in the process of planning, especially as it enables the initial deadlines to be set.

4.7 Action sheets

This system is a natural progression from activity and time scheduling. Action sheets summarise the time that the stages of the individual task should take, and contain estimates of the start and finish dates of each stage.

The example below depicts an action sheet for a wedding.

Activity number	Detail	Number of weeks in advance	Certification of completion (*initials or signature*)
1	Book church	26	
2	Book reception hall	26	
3	Send out invitations	12	
4	Receive replies	4	
5	Order food/refreshments	3	
6	Check arrangements	2	
7	The wedding day	–	

Action sheets are widely used and are often utilised in conjunction with bar charts.

4.8 Planning charts and boards

These usually show information in summary form and any required item of information may be seen at a glance. They are often used to show details of future events that affect departments (e.g. to plan staff holidays).

4.9 Diaries

Diaries are an obvious and consequently often overlooked aid to planning. They can range from simple hand-written diaries showing an individual's appointments, meetings etc through to sophisticated computerised diaries either as part of the organisation's computer network or alternatively in some form of electronic personal organiser. Diaries can also usefully be used, not just to show appointments etc, but also to highlight matters that should be followed up or chased up on a particular date. For example, suppose that you have been involved in a number of telephone discussions with a potential customer. The potential customer has indicated that he will have decided whether or not to go ahead with an order by Thursday of this week at the latest. You may wish to make a note in your diary for Wednesday to give the potential customer a telephone call in order to determine whether there is any additional information that you can provide.

Diaries are especially suited to individual employees but only if the employee ensures that all relevant details of any appointments are entered as a matter of course. This matter of full details is important because the failure to note down full and appropriate information regarding a particular appointment could have serious repercussions for the organisation, particularly if an appointment has to be rescheduled or handled by someone else. It is sensible to have a routine for making appointments and indeed to create a 'checklist for appointments'.

 Activity 3

Kate has recently joined a busy administration department in a manufacturing organisation. She is slightly shocked that the organisation seems to lack formal procedures. She feels that her job is one of 'fire-fighting'. Once one crisis is over another one arrives. She feels there is never a spare moment in the day from 9am when she arrives to 5.30pm when she goes home. She is constantly responding to so called 'urgent' requests from other people to: "just do this for me Kate please, it won't take a moment", or "this job's top priority – can you rush it through please?" Every job seems to be 'top priority'!

How will this 'Crisis Management' method of working impact on Kate? What are the consequences for her work? What time management techniques could Kate use to help organise and prioritise her workload?

5 Time management

5.1 Timetabling tasks

Work planning ensures that commitments to others are met within agreed timescales and necessitates planning and organising on the part of the organisation and the employee.

Your time needs to be properly managed if you are to work efficiently and effectively. The first way to start to organise your time is to plan your use of time.

💡 Example

Here is Joe's diary for the coming week:

May 2006				
Monday	Tuesday	Wednesday	Thursday	Friday
1	2	3	4	5
9am Meeting Mr Green	3pm Group Meeting	2.30pm Visit other site	Mum's Birthday	
7	8	9	10	11

This shows his meetings with other people but not how he will use the rest of his time.

Solution

Here is a more useful version of his diary for the same week:

May 2006	Monday	Tuesday	Wednesday	Thursday	Friday
9am	Meeting Mr Green	Record Cash	Record Cash	Record Cash	Record Cash
10am					
11am	Record Cash	Update cash book	Bank reconciliation	Finish bank reconciliation	Prepare cash flash figure
12pm					
1pm	Lunch	Lunch	Lunch	Buy card	Lunch
2pm	Record cash continued	Prepare for meeting	Site Visit	Prepare info for report	Prepare journals
3pm	Speak to Pat about new system?	Group meeting			Count petty cash
4pm					
5pm	Home early				Request cash

KAPLAN PUBLISHING

Notice how all the major tasks have been timetabled. Joe has estimated the amount of time to complete each task and blocked out that time. This ensures that Joe has sufficient time to complete tasks before the necessary **deadline**.

Activity 4

Do you allow your days to be filled with routine tasks? If so you may be neglecting longer term goals because of this. Draw three columns and in each write down one objectives or target you would like to achieve in the next 12 months. Under each objective you need to plan how it will be achieved. Set any interim targets or shorter-term deadlines that you will need to meet and what action or resources you need to succeed. (If you find setting objectives for the next 12 months too long a time-frame then try setting them on a quarterly basis).

5.2 Timing of tasks

Whatever function you perform at work, you will always have tasks, which fall into four categories:

Category		Examples
1	Daily	Recording cash received
		Recording sales invoices in sales day book
		Recording purchase invoices in purchase day book
2	Weekly	Preparing journal entries to post totals from books of prime entry to nominal ledger
3	Monthly	Sales ledger reconciliation
		Purchase ledger reconciliation
		Bank reconciliation
4	One-off	Information for reports

Joe also keeps a list of quick tasks to do at appropriate times. As he does them, he crosses them off his list.

5.3 Review of work plans

Each evening before he goes home, Joe reviews his work schedule and updates it for:

(a) things to carry over

(b) any other changes (e.g. meeting times changed).

Even if you do not have the opportunity to schedule your work, try scheduling your studies and your free time! You should find you get more out of your time.

6 Difficulties in meeting deadlines

6.1 Introduction

The syllabus area here is that you 'report anticipated difficulties in meeting deadlines to the appropriate person'. There will always be occasions, when for one reason or another the deadline or target cannot be met. Often individuals are vague regarding the information they require, which may mean wrong or incomplete information is provided. It may be that the deadline cannot be met because of problems encountered by the supplier of information. Perhaps if a student is required to provide some information, he/she might be unable to gather the information by the deadline either because of lack of sufficient working hours, or owing to personal circumstances such as doctor's/dentist's appointments.

Alternatively the problems with meeting the deadline may be due to a third party. Perhaps the information required has to be acquired from a third party. If this third party does not provide the information by the deadline you have set, then you are obviously unable to pass this information on by your deadline.

Identified below are typical examples of problems that may be encountered.

(a) Files, books, etc may be borrowed and not returned.

(b) Reference journals may not be kept up to date.

(c) Access to information may be denied due to security/confidentiality considerations.

(d) Computer systems may 'crash'.

KAPLAN PUBLISHING

(e)   International time differences may mean that offices are not open when required.

(f)   Files, books or journals may be incorrectly filed.

(g)   Wrong or insufficient information is provided.

(h)   Delays may occur because information has been archived.

Whatever the reason for not achieving the target or deadline it is vital that students understand the importance of reporting and explaining this fact.

6.2   Difficulties are promptly reported

It is tempting in any situation to put off dealing with any problems. In a business context if it appears likely that a deadline is not to be met then it is tempting to put off telling the appropriate person about this in the hope that the information can eventually be reported by the required deadline.

This really is the wrong attitude. As far as your manager or colleague, who has requested the information, is concerned it is far better that he or she knows of any possible delays at the earliest opportunity. It is therefore far better to report any possibility of non-achievement of a target at an early stage than to leave such news until the last minute. This gives the manager a chance to revise his or her plans accordingly.

The rule is therefore that if you become aware of the possibility of not being able to meet a deadline for the supply of information then this should be reported immediately. If the circumstances are eventually favourable and the information is reported by the deadline this will be an added bonus. However if the anticipated circumstances exist and the information is not available then at least the manager concerned has been able to work around the problem.

6.3   Explanation of delays

If you are unable to perform a duty by a specified deadline then not only must this fact be reported but it must be reported in an appropriate manner. Not only must politeness be considered but also businesslike behaviour.

Even if you believe that the deadline that has been set is impossible to meet, there will be nothing to be gained from an aggressive or impolite attitude towards the person requiring the information. There will be instances when deadlines are set that are earlier than is absolutely required, and provided that you give your explanation of not being able to meet that deadline in a reasonable manner then it is likely that the deadline will be extended.

In other circumstances the deadline will be vital. Again any aggressive approach by the student concerned will only heighten the displeasure of the manager at the deadline not being met. The best way to deal with any situation where a target or deadline is not achieved is to explain politely and rationally why this has not been achieved. This may be, as mentioned earlier, due to personal circumstances or due to delays from third parties.

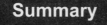

7 Summary

This chapter should help you to focus on the way you manage your own workload. How you plan, prioritise and organise both routine and non-routine work is of critical importance to how efficient and effective you will be. Now that you have read the chapter you should be aware of the importance of anticipating problems before they arise and asking for assistance where necessary. Identifying any weaknesses in your own skills, level of experience, or ability to meet deadlines is critical to working effectively as a member of a team.

Answers to chapter activities

Activity 1

Possible routine tasks for someone working in, for example, purchase ledger, could include:

- opening and distributing the post
- taking telephone calls from suppliers
- processing supplier invoices
- posting supplier invoices to purchase ledger
- filing all invoices received
- maintaining up to date records of the outstanding creditor position and when payments are due.

Possible non-routine tasks could include:

- provide up to date aged creditor analysis to new investor
- raise sales invoices when colleague off sick.

Activity 2

	Job	Importance ranking	Urgency ranking
1	Bank cheques	9	9
2	Order stationery	2	5
3	Make dental appointment	1	1
4	Send out customer invoices	5	8
5	File supplier invoices	3	2
6	Open post	5	8
7	Make coffee	1	1
8	Holiday application form	1	2
9	Report to Director due next week	10	4
10	Memo to manager re broken window catch	3	7
11	Deal with irate window cleaner	2	10

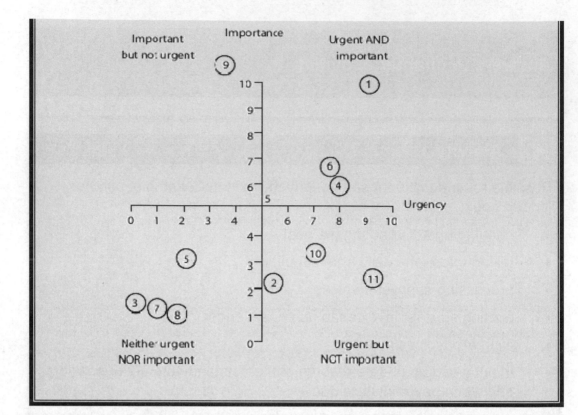

Activity 3

Kate appears to have always respond to others demands upon her time and has little control over planning her own time or work. The likely impact of this method of working on Kate is that it will be stressful and unsatisfying. The consequences for her work are that it is likely to deteriorate in quality and important deadlines may be missed as others encroach upon her time.

It is important that Kate learns strict time management techniques such as daily lists and action plans. She needs to prioritise her tasks perhaps in negotiation with those supplying her with the tasks. To do this she need to communicate very firmly and clearly with those supplying her with work. Next time someone asks her to do something that is supposed to be 'top priority' she must ascertain exactly when the work is required by and firmly negotiate a reasonable deadline. In this way colleagues may learn to respect that she is a busy person who has other demands upon her time than simply responding to their demands.

What people tend to notice is that they regularly do the urgent but not important jobs before the important but not urgent jobs. This is quite wrong. Prioritisation is all about ensuring important jobs are done first. Therefore the jobs that fall into the top part of the graph - the important jobs, are those that should be focussed on. In this case, job number 9 the report to a director due next week is the job that should be focused on, bearing in mind any other deadlines that must be met. Of course other people's needs (such as the irate window cleaner) will get in the way of achieving this aim but as a general rule you should focus on the important jobs first, such as the report to the director and banking cheques, slotting in any urgent jobs as best you can. Yet how often do you get to the office, make a coffee, fill in your holiday application form and order some new stationery all because you think they are quick, simple jobs that will only take a minute!

Whilst it would not be practical to draw a Time Management Grid every day to help prioritise tasks, it gives useful practice in learning how to prioritise tasks, especially when under time pressure or during busy periods of the year.

Activity 4

	Objective / target 1	Objective / target 2	Objective / target 3
Overall goal:			
How?			
Action required?			
Interim targets?			
3 months?			
6 months?			
12 months?			
Resources required?			

Working relationships

6

Introduction

The efficient running of organisations requires that all the members of the organisation work together towards the achievement of the organisation's objectives. This working together requires the adequate understanding of what others are doing. It requires a high level of coordination and control, and fundamentally it requires communication, which is efficient and effective.

KNOWLEDGE
3.2 Identify the impact that the non-completion of work can have on your colleagues.
3.3 Resolve or refer conflicts or dissatisfaction within your working environment.

CONTENTS
1 Co-ordination
2 Communication
3 Methods of communication
4 Confidential information
5 Interpersonal skills
6 Teams
7 Handling disagreements and conflicts

1 Co-ordination

1.1 Co-ordination and communication

As we have already noted, an appropriate organisation structure will ensure that all sections of the business are pursuing common objectives and clearly defined job descriptions will improve appreciation of the interrelatedness of tasks and should prevent overlapping or areas of responsibility being missed. Standard instructions and procedures are a way of reducing the risk of conflicting practices within the company.

However, your role and responsibilities are an integral part of the organisation's structure and cannot be treated in isolation from other people. Your colleagues will have joint objectives and goals, which will necessitate pooling resources, information and efforts.

Any business activity is in part about ensuring the co-ordination of organisational and individual endeavour, and of co-ordinating the work of individuals and teams. Some activities will be dependent on the successful and timely completion of other activities so you need to be aware of your own requirements as well as the plans and deadlines of others in the organisation.

Poor co-ordination is often at the heart of complaints from customers or colleagues e.g., two departments giving different information. It can cause workflow problems if work arrives unplanned or later than planned from another unit. This can cause conflict between departments with one blaming the other for the problem instead of both working together and co-operating to perform effectively and efficiently.

In any organisation, the communication of information is necessary to achieve co-ordination.

1.2 Social skills

You will see that social skills are important to the organisation, as well as to the individuals employed and this is what we mean by working relations. There will be jobs where co-operation with colleagues is highly essential. It would, of course, be no good to have a large number of employees who all argue and disagree with each other. Apart from the disruption caused to each other, the organisation would also suffer since the amount of work carried out would probably be very small and perhaps even counter-productive.

What is meant by social skills? It means the ways in which we discuss work related matters with others, or obtain information from them. You will be aware of the situation when you want to take some annual leave and need to ask your supervisor whether you can have the time off when you require it. The supervisor may tell you right away, ask you to put it in writing or need to ask the boss later. What is important is the way you 'get on' with your supervisor and perhaps the way in which they recognise you. If the approach is right, then you might be told right away there are no problems, even though there may be some particular way in which you should go about it. Your social skills or the way you put the question over is important, not only to you – especially if you want time off – but to the organisation because it is in this way that a certain amount of confidence builds up between you and the supervisor.

It is not unknown to find a clash of personality between individuals in a line organisation, and it is up to the senior officer in the organisation to take the appropriate action. Whilst there can be no hard and fast rules on what should be done, the interests of the organisation must take priority, although there may be certain circumstances where the individual's interests should be taken into consideration.

When dealing with other people in your organisation you should be as courteous and polite as when dealing with external customers.

1.3 Contractual and legal relationships

Employment is a legal relationship with your employer. There are underlying duties of to your employer under your contract of employment, including:

- **Duty of care** – there is implied into every contract of employment a duty that the employee performs his/her contract with proper care.

- **Duty of co-operation** – even where the employer promulgates a rulebook containing instructions for the execution of the work, the employee is under an obligation not to construe the rules in a way designed to defeat the efficiency of the employer's business.

- **Duty of obedience** – in the absence of express provisions an employee is required to carry out all reasonable and lawful orders of the employer. Some orders clearly do not require obedience e.g. falsify sales records on employer's instructions; drive an unroadworthy vehicle, which may lead to his prosecution under the Road Traffic Acts.

- **Loyal service** – this duty is to use all reasonable steps to advance his employer's business within the sphere of his employment and not to do anything which might injure the employer's business.

1.4   Equal Opportunities Legislation

'Equal opportunities' is a term describing the belief that there should be an equal chance for all workers to apply to be selected for jobs, to be trained and promoted in employment and have that employment terminated fairly. There are two main reasons for adopting equal opportunities policies:

(i)   it is morally wrong to treat parts of the population as inferior or inadequate

(ii)   organisations do not benefit from excluding any potential source of talent.

The legislation on equal opportunities is made up of several Acts:

*   **The Sex Discrimination Act of 1975** renders it unlawful to make any form of discrimination in employment affairs because of marital status or sex.

*   **The Race Relations Act of 1976** ensures that there should be no discrimination on the grounds of colour, nationality, ethnic origin or race

*   **The Equal Pay Act 1970** is concerned with equality of pay and related matters. The Act aims to ensure that where men and women are employed in 'like work' or 'work of equal value' or 'rated as equivalent', they will receive the same basic pay.

*   **The Disability Discrimination Act 1995** provides for disabled people not to be discriminated against in a variety of circumstances including employment.

*   **The Rehabilitation of Offenders Act 1974** provides that a conviction, other than one involving imprisonment for more than 30 months, may become erased if the offender commits no further serious offences during the rehabilitation period.

Discrimination may operate in all kinds of areas including sex, sexuality and marital status, race and colour, religion, politics, disability and conviction of a criminal offence. Forward-looking organisations will have a positive attitude to equal opportunities and operate non-discriminating procedures in all aspects of personnel management, including recruitment and selection, advertisements, access to training and promotion, disciplinary procedures, redundancy and dismissal.

As an employee you also have responsibilities under the equal opportunities legislation not to discriminate or show prejudice against people on the grounds of sex, race or disability.

1.5   Carrying out instructions

An employee who will not carry out instructions will not be welcomed by most firms. The instructions are given so that the work to be performed can be understood and will fit into the total workload of the department. Failure to carry out instructions may:

(a)   delay a piece of work needed urgently by a customer

(b)   completely wreck the rest of the work performed by everyone else

(c)   endanger lives or health of other employees or customers (e.g.by operating a machine without following instructions or smoking in 'non-smoking' areas).

Employees should expect their employers to give proper instructions at the right time, in the right manner and in the right place. Failure to do so can mean that the employees might lose pay bonuses because they are unable to complete the work within a prescribed time. It can also lead to poor morale due to workers arguing about what should be done, rather than being fully aware of their commitments.

In addition, instructions to protect employees' physical well-being which are not given properly, or not given at all, can result in disability or even death.

1.6   Asking for clarification when necessary

It is possible for instructions genuinely to be misunderstood or for completely wrong instructions to be given. If this happens to you at any time, you should ask for clarification of the instructions. Simply to carry on with the job when the instructions are genuinely not clear, or where they are obviously wrong, can cause all sorts of problems. Your employer or supervisor would therefore expect you to question the instructions in such cases.

Of course it is possible to be obstinate and obstructive by deliberately trying to misinterpret instructions. You must be careful to ensure that your manager or supervisor understands your proper concern at the lack of clear instructions and does not mistakenly assume that you are being unnecessarily awkward.

If you are ever unclear about instructions that you have been given you should always check them with the appropriate person.

1.7   Asking for assistance

If an individual feels that they are not up to the demands of a particular job or that a deadline cannot be met then this is likely to be due to either a lack of time, or a lack of skills or a lack of experience. A lack of time is almost impossible to deal with unless large amounts of overtime are to be worked. Lack of skills or experience however can be overcome if assistance is sought.

Skills – if the inability to perform a particular task is due a lack of skills or necessary knowledge for that task then there should be no embarrassment about admitting this fact. For example suppose that you have never before performed a bank reconciliation and a stand-in supervisor in the department has suddenly asked you to prepare the monthly bank reconciliation by the end of tomorrow. Obviously this task is impossible for you. There is no point in attempting it alone as this will simply be an unproductive use of the organisation's time. However it is likely that colleagues in your department, or indeed the supervisor, may be able to instruct you in exactly how to perform a bank reconciliation. Therefore the only practical option for you is to seek assistance.

Lack of experience – it is often the case that an individual is probably capable of performing a task but does not have the confidence to go ahead with the task because of a lack of experience. Perhaps it is the first time that that individual has been required to perform a particular task. In such instances both informal and formal support can be sought. Colleagues may well be able to encourage an individual to feel confident of performing the task. However if the situation is such that an individual truly believes himself or herself to be incapable of performing the task then it is probably most appropriate to discuss this matter with the supervisor or manager.

1.8 Informal and formal assistance

Many people find it much easier to approach a colleague to ask for help – informal assistance – with a problem than to approach a more senior member of staff. This might well be appropriate if it is within the organisation's policies, the colleague is fully skilled in the area concerned and the colleague has the time, ability and inclination to help. In many cases this will be the most satisfactory way of dealing with a problem.

Formal assistance means approaching the supervisor or manager of the department to ask for help in dealing with a lack of skills. Once it has been realised that no training has been given in that particular area then the individual will not be allocated that task again until they are trained.

2.1 Introduction

Communication is the basis of our relationships with other people. It is the means whereby people in an organisation exchange information regarding the operations of the enterprise. It is the interchange of ideas, facts and emotions by two or more persons. To be effective, the manager needs information to carry out management functions and activities. All organisations have formal, acknowledged, and often specified communication channels. There will be lists of people who are to attend briefings or meetings, and distribution lists for minutes of meetings or memos. There will be procedures for telling people of decisions or changes, and for circulating information received from outside the organisation.

Communication takes place between various employees of a business and the outside world, in such forms as:

(a)   reports and dividend payments to shareholders

(b)   invoices and correspondence to customers

(c)   orders, payments and queries to suppliers.

For the present purpose, our immediate concern is communication within a business, where the need arises because of:

- day-to-day and periodic control needs

- the incidence of unplanned change

- the introduction of planned change

- the usual interaction in the normal work situation.

2.2 Communication process

Communication is the process of passing information and understanding from one person to another. The communication process involves six basic elements: sender (encoder), message, channel, receiver (decoder), noise, and feedback. You can improve your communication skills by becoming aware of these elements and how they contribute to successful communication. Communication can break down at any one of these elements. The process of communication can be modelled as shown in the following diagram.

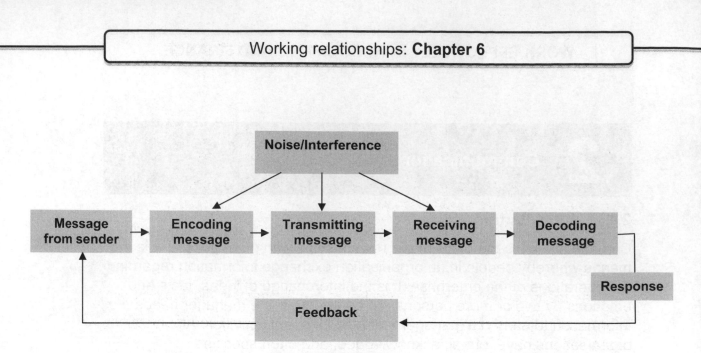

A sender will initiate the communication process. When the meaning has been decided, a channel for transmitting the messages to the receiver is selected and the message is put into words or images. When the receiver has heard the 'message' then they have to 'decode' it to make sure they understand what is being said. For example, the sender may use 'jargon' which the receiver may not understand.

Sometimes the response may result in action taking the form of the receiver asking for clarification on respect of something they do not understand or asking for additional information

The final stage of the process is feedback, which can consist for example of the receiver indicating that they understood the message, or providing information.

Within the communication process it is also important to note the problem of 'noise': anything in the environment that hinders the transmission of the message is significant. Noise can arise from many sources, e.g. factors as diverse as loud machinery, status differentials between sender and receiver, distractions of pressure at work or emotional upsets. The effective communicator must ensure that noise does not interfere with successful transmission of the message.

2.3   Noise/interference

🔍 Definition

'Noise' is full or partial loss of communication. It can arise at the collecting and measuring point, or there can be errors or omissions in transmission and/or misinterpretation or misunderstanding, or blatant disregard of communication.

The two principal types of noise are verbal and technical.

Verbal noise is the misunderstanding of words. Examples are:

(a)   the misspelling or omission of an important word in a communication, so as to obscure or alter its meaning

(b)   technical persons (such as accountants, who are some of the worst offenders) using jargon that is incomprehensible to non-technical persons

(c)   the incorrect use of English, written in a style that is difficult to follow.

Technical noise is created by the information itself during communication. Examples are:

(a)   in response to a request for a simple piece of information, a voluminous report may be prepared obscuring the vital information (accountants' monthly reports frequently have this failing)

(b)   a message is left that is not sufficiently clear to convey its meaning when its intended recipient returns

(c)   damage to an organisation's communications centre, such as its telephone exchange, prevents information from being transmitted clearly.

Failure to transmit information can have serious consequences on a company's operations. Some noise can be reduced, if not overcome, by using more than one channel of communication, so that if a message fails to get through by one channel, it may succeed by another. For example, a managing director may need the latest stock figures. To confirm the information from the accountant, the figures from sales and production may be analysed personally to find the relevant stock figures.

2.4   Formal communication channels

Formal communication channels are normally established as part of the organisation's structure. In a hierarchical structure the channels are largely vertical chains designed to allow effective communication between managers and subordinates. Organisational communication establishes a pattern of formal communication channels to carry information vertically and horizontally. (The organisational chart displays these channels.) The channel is the path a message follows from the sender to the receiver.

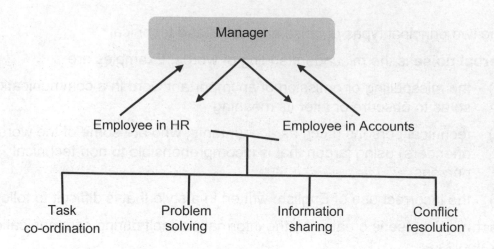

- Managers use downward channels as a basis for giving specific job instructions, policy decisions, guidance and resolution of queries. Such information can help clarify operational goals, provide a sense of direction and give subordinates data related to their performance. Downward communication also helps link levels of the hierarchy by providing a basis for co-ordinated activity.

- Employees use upward channels to send messages to managers. Upward communication provides management with feedback from employees on results achieved and problems encountered. It creates a channel from which management can gauge organisational climate and deal with problem areas, such as grievances or low productivity, before they become major issues.

- Horizontal channels are used when communicating across departmental lines, with suppliers, or with customers. Four of the most important reasons for lateral communication are:

  - **task co-ordination** – department heads may meet periodically to discuss how each department is contributing to organisational objectives

  - **problem-solving** – members of a department may meet to discuss how they will handle a threatened budget cut

  - **information sharing** – members of one department may meet with the members of another department to explain some new information or study

  - **conflict resolution** – members of one department may meet to discuss a problem, e.g. duplication of activities in the department and some other department.

KAPLAN PUBLISHING

2.5 Informal communication networks

In every organisation there are informal communication networks as well as the formal channels. This is often referred to as 'the grapevine', which has been defined as 'the network of social relations that arises spontaneously as people associate with one another. It is an expression of people's natural motivation to communicate'.

Grapevine activity is likely to flourish in many common situations, for example:

- where there is a lack of information about a situation and people try to fill in the gaps as best they can

- where there is insecurity in the situation

- where there is a personal interest in a situation e.g. when a supervisor disciplines a friend, people may well gossip about it

- where there is personal animosity in a situation and people seek to gain advantage by the spreading of rumours

- where there is new information that people wish to spread quickly.

Though the grapevine can pose a threat to management, it can also be useful as a means of making unofficial announcements, 'off-the-record' statements or intentional leaks of future plans.

2.6 Attributes of effective communication

The main attributes of effective communication are promptness and accuracy.

Promptness – if information is essential then it is likely to be urgent. It is therefore important that such information is passed on at the earliest possible opportunity.

In respect of messages, if at all possible you should try to identify how urgent the message is, for example, depending on the situation by asking the following questions:

'Jane Smith is in a meeting at the moment and will not be out until 3.00 pm. Would you like me to arrange for this message to be passed to her in the meeting?'

'Jack Little is in the building but I'm not sure where. Would you like me to arrange for him to be paged?'

'Peter Green is currently travelling to a meeting. Would you like his mobile telephone number?'

If the information is contained in a report or in some form of written document, then often couriers are used to ensure that they reach their destination that day or as early as possible the next.

Accuracy – accurate transmission of information is clearly vital. For example suppose that a client leaves a telephone message with you changing his meeting with your manager from 3.00pm until 4.15pm. If you tell your manager that the meeting is about 4.30pm this is likely to leave the client waiting for some considerable amount of time.

Always ensure you read back any messages taken to the person you are talking to. In this way telephone numbers etc can be checked.

Activity 1

The following fax has just been received in the accounts department. It has been passed to you, the accounts clerk, as the most appropriate person available.

To: J Patel, Quotations Manager

From: Peter Allan, Sales Manager, East Sussex Materials Ltd

Further to our telephone conversation this morning I am prepared to drop the price of raw material XX5 to £2.42 per kg for the project that you explained to me this morning. I hope this is satisfactory.

Consider what the possible implications might be if you delay passing on this information to the quotations manager.

2.7   Overcoming barriers to communication

A barrier to communication is anything that prevents, or may potentially prevent, communication from being effective.

Some general rules to ensure communication is effective are:

- avoid communication overload

- ensure the right information gets to the right person at the right time

- agree and confirm priorities and deadlines for receipt of information

- keep communication simple

- develop empathy with 'listeners'

- confirm, by repeating back, what has been said

- confirm that what information you have given has been understood.

3 Methods of communication

3.1 Oral communication – face-to-face and telephone

For the rapid interchange of information between people, the principal method of communication is the spoken word. Oral communication is preferable for emotive issues and persuasion since it has the advantage of immediate feedback. It is, however, time consuming and, unless recorded, there can be uncertainty about what was said.

Telephone – for many years the telephone has been most important both for internal and external communications. It is usually used when individuals are not on the same site, or when the conversation may be very short. The telephone can now be used for conference meetings, whereby everyone present at each end of the telephone can hear comments made by the other parties. This means people can convene meetings in two locations at the same time and carry out discussions.

Face-to-face discussions may be used where people need to exchange/give/obtain information quickly, and or obtain documents. This form of communication is appropriate when working relationships need to be developed or negotiation/persuasion has to take place.

Meetings can be organised to include various departments, or may include outside representatives such as shareholders. They may include various levels of management and can be convened to provide information or discuss a specific topic e.g. year end accounts. In formal meetings minutes may be taken.

Advantages of oral communication	Disadvantages of oral communication
There is the personal touch of seeing the face and/or hearing the voice.	There is no permanent record, so disagreement can easily arise as to what was said.
There is instant feedback with the opportunity to respond quickly to questions of misunderstanding and disagreement.	Vocabulary shrinkage occurs, in that we use only 66% of our full vocabulary when communicating orally – the full vocabulary is available to us only when writing.
Because of the strong personal aspect, it is a good persuasive medium encouraging people to take a certain course of action.	We do not have the facility, as with writing, to go back, cancel out and replace an earlier sentence because we wish to amend its meaning.

> The message can be unique to you as an individual – no-one else is likely to select your mix of words or emphasise the same key phrases.

3.2 Written communication – letters, memos and word-processed documents

Written methods of communication of all sorts – letters, memos, bulletins, files, circulars – are the norm in many companies. The dominant characteristic of many managers' working day is paperwork and meetings. They do have the advantage that being in permanent or hard copy form they are less open to misinterpretation. With meetings, for instance, formal minutes may be taken, circulated and agreed to as the definitive written evidence of the meeting. Written methods of communication can be very flexibly used. When trying to reach a number of workers in one place, notice-boards are often used, typically to announce meetings, job vacancies, health and safety notices, details of company social events and similar matters which are not of crucial significance

Most written communications will be word-processed documents nowadays with the exception of memos that are written by hand and placed in the internal mailing system. **Memos** can also be sent by electronic mail on the computer network. They are most useful where the same information has to be given to a number of people e.g. details of the date, time, location of a meeting.

Letters provide a written record and information of matters discussed. Used mainly for external communication.

Notes – you may need to write notes for a talk or a presentation. Other occasions when note taking is required might be in the preparation of a report or in connection with a meeting or a telephone call. Whatever the context, notes should suit their purpose and be neither too detailed that they resemble an essay nor too compressed that their meaning is lost.

Notes that are going to be used very soon after they have been written down can afford to be more condensed than notes, which will have to wait before they are written in a more acceptable form. Telephone messages tend to suffer from brevity and, with each hour that passes, recollection of the conversation will fade.

Reports may be for internal or external circulation and can take a variety of forms. Reports may contain data, graphs, complex facts and points for and against a variety of situations. This form of communication allows people to study the content in their own time. Some reports are required by law, while other reports may detail progress made in respect of a particular project.

Word-processed documents – word processing programs are now common in the workplace and used to produce a wide variety of written documents, often in a 'house style'. Standard letters and memos can be produced from template files set up on the computer. Mail-merge facilities enable a word processed letter file to import names and addresses from a database and print out a batch for sending out.

Word-processed documents can have sophisticated page layouts and tables. They can import graphics and embody colour elements for illustrative purposes. They are also used in the form of transaction documents, such as payslips, invoices sent to customers, purchase orders sent to suppliers and works orders sent to the factory, day book listings or standard letters. Large numbers of these documents are produced, perhaps in electronic form and displayed on screens or perhaps as 'paperwork'.

Bulletins and newsletters usually provide details on major changes or events that will affect the organisation and may appear in the local or national press, for example a move to a new site or the creation of new jobs.

3.3   Visual communication

Visual methods are preferable where it is necessary for the eye to assist the ear; where the message can be made more vivid, or where distance, environmental or personal factors preclude the use of speech. Examples include films, videos, graphs, traffic signals and sign language.

Graphic displays of data can be an effective way of communicating. For example, sales data comparing this year with last year. Data can often appear more meaningful when presented in this way rather than just a list of figures.

Films and slides – allow information to be absorbed in an easily digestible way. Also, if entertaining and well put together, individuals are more likely to listen, concentrate and remember what is being said.

3.4   Electronic methods – fax, e-mail and video conferencing

More and more offices are increasingly reliant on a range of electronic communication equipment. Larger businesses link computers through the telephone network using modems leading to the use of electronic mail and computers 'speaking' to each other, some accessing databanks. Personal computers are being arranged in networks; fax machines, e-mail, value added networks (VANs) and dedicated satellite communication systems are becoming commonplace.

Fax (facsimile) – allows images of documents to be transmitted and then reproduced. It can handle photographs, hand-written notes, drawings, diagrams, charts, etc with no specialist skill to transmit. It is also easy to send the same document to many recipients. Developments include an interface between fax and the computer so that the latter is able to hold, store and process fax transmissions.

The system can 'read' the incoming fax material and relay it to the individual addressee (by displaying on the screen of the terminal).

The development of fax cards for fitting inside desktop and portable personal computers has eliminated much of the need for specialised fax machines. It is now possible to send and receive fax messages using a laptop PC and mobile telephone anywhere in the world.

E-mail – electronic mail is very popular as a form of communication that uses the Internet.

The following are hints on what to do and what not to do when using e-mail.

- E-mail is meant to be one of the quickest ways to communicate. It is much more efficient than a letter or even a phone call. Some people receive hundreds of e-mails a day, so keep e-mail short and to the point. But be aware – rushed messages can lead to bad grammar and miscommunication.

- You can send e-mail by following three simple steps:

  1 Enter the recipient's e-mail address in the To field.

  2 Type your message in the large text box. Avoid using a string of capital letters in your correspondence unless absolutely necessary. This is the online equivalent of SHOUTING!

  3 Click on the Send button.

You can also use several options when addressing your message, such as:

1 Put additional or secondary recipients in the Cc (carbon copy) field.

2 When you are sending a message to many people, a long delivery list may appear at the top of the message. This can annoy readers. It also can make your message seem like junk mail. To hide the distribution list from all recipients, use the Bcc (blind carbon copy) field.

3 If you have created nicknames in the Address Book, you can just type the nickname in the appropriate field. In order to send your message to multiple recipients, separate each recipient by a comma. For example: nickname1, nickname2, recipient3@host.domain.

- Although the **Subject** is an optional field, it is a good idea to enter one. Your recipients may receive many e-mail messages, perhaps even several from you alone. The subject helps distinguish between the different messages.

- You can attach a file to your message by clicking **Attach**. The Attachment area will be opened in a new window. Click **Browse**... and search for the file or type the full path name of the file you wish to attach. Once found, press the **Upload file** button and the file name will appear in the Attachment List. In order to remove an already attached file, select the file from the Attachment List and press the **Remove** button. Finally, press the **OK** button to return to Compose window.

  The file you attach can be of any type, for example: a sound file, an image or even a spreadsheet. Adding attachments to your message can be done at any time while composing the message. All files are scanned for viruses before they are attached to a message. If a file contains a virus that cannot be cleared by the virus scanning software, you will be unable to attach it to the message.

- You can check the spelling of your message by choosing the language from the selection list and pressing the **Spell Checker** button. The Spelling area will be opened in a new window. The first word that was not found in the Spelling Dictionary will appear on the top of the page marked by red text. You will see a list of possible suggestions. Select the appropriate replacement from the list or write the replacement yourself in the Change to edit box. Then press the Change button to accept the change or the Ignore button to disregard it. This process will continue until the end of the message is reached.

- Pressing the Cancel button, before completion, will discontinue the spelling process.

- The sender of an e-mail message is not always apparent to the recipient simply by looking at the sender's address. It is good practice to sign your e-mail with your name and what company you are with, if applicable. You may want to include your e-mail address as well. Most e-mail services allow you to write a signature that will automatically be attached to each message you send.

Video conferencing is increasingly used as a medium whereby meetings are convened in two locations simultaneously.

4.1 Types of confidential information

You may handle information that is clearly confidential, such as payroll details. Some information may not appear to be confidential at first sight but could cause embarrassment or problems internally or externally if revealed, so it is best always to err on the side of discretion. For example:

(a) reports on purchases of new machinery whose introduction might lead to fewer jobs

(b) details of price rises not yet sent to customers

(c) news of changes in key personnel not yet communicated to customers and suppliers.

When dealing with customers and suppliers, you must also respect their own right to confidentiality. For instance, do not reveal details of a customer's account or type or level of purchases to another customer.

Remember that, if someone appears to be asking for confidential information or for information, which is none of their concern, it is always best to refer them to your supervisor.

In certain limited circumstances students may become aware of confidential information that needs to be passed to the appropriate staff member. This means that it should not be discussed in any circumstances other than with the person for whom the information was meant. The information should not therefore be discussed in passing with colleagues, managers or in social situations. Confidentiality should always be maintained where considered necessary. Your organisation's affairs and those of its clients are confidential and should not be disclosed to others unless the circumstances are appropriate.

If you are leaving a confidential message for someone who is not available it should be written down, and placed in a sealed envelope, marked 'Private and Confidential Addressee Only'.

Alternatively if you have to send a memo, letter or report, which contains confidential information, then you should ensure it is marked private and confidential and placed in a sealed envelope that is similarly marked.

4.2 Organisational procedures

It is each individual's responsibility to ensure that they are fully aware of the organisation's rules and procedures regarding confidential information. It is equally important that an individual follows them strictly.

For example if the organisation's policy is that documents marked as 'confidential' are kept under lock and key then it is important that such documents are stored in a locked storage cabinet or desk each night. This is reasonably easy to remember to do. It is perhaps harder to remember to keep the information locked away whenever the individual is not using it and is not in their office or at their workstation. Such information should not, under any circumstances, be left unattended on a desk.

When confidential information is considered, individuals should be aware that they are only likely to be able to access confidential information if they have been allocated a particular password. If an individual is given a password in order to access confidential information then under no circumstances should they tell anybody else what their password is.

Disclosure of information could damage the company if it fell foul of the data protection legislation and caused embarrassing publicity or helped a competitor by allowing sensitive information to be accessed by outsiders or non-related employees.

4.3 Handling confidential information

The increasing use of computers in all aspects of business has meant that increasingly large amounts of information about individuals are now kept by various organisations. For you to perform some of your tasks it may be necessary to obtain and keep confidential information. This is a great responsibility and should not be taken lightly.

There will be rules and procedures for compliance with the Data Protection Act and with the copyright laws, and to avoid any action that might reflect badly on the reputation of the company.

Under the terms of the Data Protection Act, the need for privacy is recognised by the requirements that all data should be held for clearly designated purposes. Accuracy and integrity must be maintained and data must be open to inspection. Only legitimate parties can access data and information must be secured against alteration, accidental loss or deliberate damage. Furthermore, the Act states that data must be obtained fairly, to precise specifications and must not be kept for longer than required.

Copyright law covers books of all kinds, sound recordings, film and broadcasts, computer programs, dramatic and musical works. Modern software packages are complex and costly to produce, but are often easy to copy and distribute. Manufacturers are increasingly bringing prosecutions to try to reduce the number of pirate copies of their software. There are steep penalties for companies prosecuted for software theft – unlimited damages, legal costs and the cost of legitimising the software.

However, not all information at work is covered by legislation. There will be times when you are told something and asked to 'keep it to yourself', either by a colleague, your supervisor or a visitor. Sometimes this will be in the context of a message you may have to pass on, but at other times it may be in the form of a confidence, which is entrusted to you. It is vital that you keep your word and do not pass it on to others at the earliest opportunity.

Working as part of a team will inevitably mean that you must pass information on to other members of the team. This must always be done accurately and promptly.

4.4 Copyright law

It is highly likely that when supplying information a student will use another individual's ideas or information. Is this a breach of copyright law?

Copyright law covers books of all kinds, sound recordings, films and broadcasts computer programmes, dramatic and musical works, etc. Is it possible to legally photocopy or manually copy such information?

It is normally quite acceptable for an individual to copy a few pages of the work of another person. That other person may have signalled his copyright by the international symbol of ©; however, it is still quite acceptable to copy such works in small amounts either for personal or business usage.

Unless you intend to copy an entire book or reproduce a copyright article for the entire organisation, it is unlikely that any copyright law would be infringed.

5 Interpersonal skills

5.1 Definition

Interpersonal skills can sometimes be called interactive, face-to-face or social skills used in establishing and maintaining relationships between people. If you can answer yes to any of these questions, it indicates your power is based on interpersonal skills.

- Do you have a sense of relationship – rapport – with other people?

- Are you an 'active listener? Do you make sure you have understood the other person's point of view? Do you make it clear to them that you understand and empathise?

- Do you avoid being either passive or aggressive in formal or informal discussions with others in the organisation?

- Can you persuade or influence another person?

- Are you aware that people admire you in some respects, and do others copy you?

- Do people want to be with you at informal meetings?

5.2 Steps to improve your people skills

Being able to manage your relationships at work, so that they have the effect you want, is a prerequisite of optimum performance. Key interpersonal skills are the building blocks of relationships:

1 **Self-management** – when we think of people skills, we usually think of them in relation to other people, rather than how we handle ourselves, and yet most of us realise that we are better or worse at relating to people depending on our 'mood' or attitude. The reason for the 'mood' is the way we are choosing to react to a particular situation; we can learn to choose consciously, and use a mood to our advantage in any situation. We all know the difference it makes to a working day when we wake up feeling good, rather than feeling that it is 'going to be one of those days'. Make a conscious effect to seek the benefits of each situation, to enjoy the process as well as the end results of work. What we tell ourselves is very powerful in affecting our state; we can talk ourselves 'up' or 'down'.

2 **Building rapport** – the word 'rapport' comes from the French word that means carrying something back; rapport is about actively making sure that we have some shared message that we both send and receive. We can build rapport by being aware of the non-verbal messages we communicate. If we make eye contact, use a friendly tone of voice, turn towards them, look relaxed and smile, we create the impression of being someone easy to deal with.

3 **Giving attention** – paying attention is not the same as listening, and if we want to develop good people skills, we need to learn to pay close attention to people. When someone is really paying attention we feel not just that they have listened, but that they have understood where we are coming from and what we really mean.

To pay full attention requires:

- listening with your ears – you pick up the words someone is saying

- listening with the inner ear – we pick up the tone of voice, the meaning behind the words, the emphasis and hesitations

- attending with your eyes – how the person's body language supports or negates what they are saying

- attending with your guts – this is the intuitive level, we get a sense of something not being communicated

- attending with your heart – we view the person sympathetically rather than judgmentally, and get a sense of what it is like from their point of view.

4   **Recognising and working with differences** – most of us have not been brought up to value other people for their difference, often we have to learnt to judge others because of it. By finding out how others are different from us, we gain very useful information to help us to deal with them more effectively. We can find out about other people's approaches or perspectives by asking 'what' and 'how' questions; e.g. How did you do that? What prompted you to handle it in that way? How is that important for you? If you were left to your own devices, how would you deal with this? Once you have found out what really matters to the other person, you can make your communication with them much more effective.

5   **Conveying your message clearly** – if we want to be sure our message is received correctly, it is important that we are sure what our message is! You may wish to tell people about new working practices, but additionally, your tone of voice, body language, choice of words will tell them what sort of person you are, what you feel about your overt message, how you operate in the world and what you think and feel about your listeners. Being clear in our own minds what our message is, and what we want the listener to do or feel as a result helps to ensure that the right message is conveyed.

6   **Using feedback** – this is a term that describes a loop of action and reaction. The most common feedback we receive is that which is given unconsciously, it is the immediate response or reaction to what we have done or said. If you are not sure of someone's reaction, asking them is the simplest way of finding out, but we need to guide the feedback, as most people are not good at giving useful information about their reactions and will tend to rationalise or justify their responses.

7 **Working in a team** – good team skills include respect for each other's viewpoints, sharing information, mutual support, and presenting a coherent front.

8 **Dealing with conflict** – when you strongly disagree with someone, it is hard to maintain a good working relationship, as we tend to equate the disagreement with the person. It is important in dealing with conflict to step back and assess the situation objectively. Identify the reason for the conflict (misunderstanding, different approaches, different interests?) and where possible find common ground. Changing the language of discussion can improve the situation; notice the difference in feeling these pairs of comments produce:

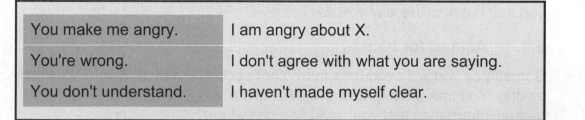

You make me angry.	I am angry about X.
You're wrong.	I don't agree with what you are saying.
You don't understand.	I haven't made myself clear.

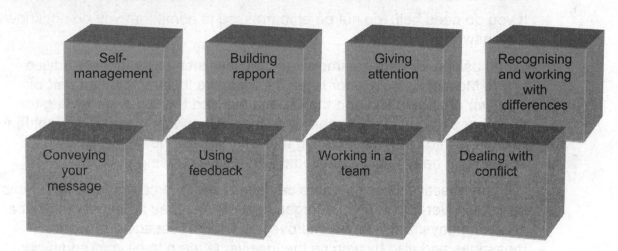

5.3 Responding to requests

To be able to communicate effectively you must have the ability to:

- pass on information accurately and without delay so that all concerned are aware of the situation and the correct action can be taken

- talk to a wide range of people with whom you have had little or no previous contact

- converse with your colleagues in a way which will promote and maintain a harmonious working atmosphere

- interpret non-verbal communication gestures and their meanings · put people at their ease.

Even if you can schedule a lot of your own work, you will inevitably be asked to do things by your supervisor or other managers. In any job, you will have to do things you do not like. The important thing is to accept that everyone is in the same position and so you should try to carry out unwelcome tasks without complaining.

The way you act is very important. Do you appear disinterested when other people ask you to do something or do you appear attentive? Do you interrupt or do you let the other person finish first?

When dealing with colleagues, it is important to think about not only what you say but also the way you say it.

5.4 Asking for help

Sometimes you will need help from other people, but think carefully before asking. You may waste other people's time if you ask them for simple factual information that you could find elsewhere.

If you do need help, do not be embarrassed to admit that you do not know the answer.

When asking for help it is important that you listen to the help or advice given. Most of us have poor listening skills. We listen to the first part of what we are being told and then spend the next few seconds waiting for the other person to stop speaking so that we can say the next thought that has come into our heads. During this latter part of the other person's speech, we have totally switched off from what is being said.

Without effective listening, there can be no effective communication. It has been discovered that people forget most of what they have heard within a couple of days. This can be improved by better messages, repeated messages and also by helping the receiver to learn to be a more efficient listener.

Among the many ideas for better listening are the following:

(a) concentrate on what is being said, not on the person saying it

(b) ask for something to be repeated if you do not understand

(c) try to concentrate on the meaning of the message

(d) do not become emotionally involved

(e) remember that thoughts are quicker than words and you can evaluate what is being said without missing anything

(f) do not take many notes, just the key points.

Listening is not the same as hearing. It involves a more conscious assimilation of information and requires attentiveness on the part of the interviewer. Failure to listen properly to what someone is saying will mean that probing questions (in an interview) may become a worthless exercise. In preparing to listen you should ask 'What new things can I learn from this person?'

Barriers to listening include the following:

- scoring points – relating everything you hear to your own experience

- mind-reading

- rehearsing – practising your next lines in your head

- cherry-picking – listening for a key piece of information then switching off

- daydreaming – you can think faster than people can talk and there is a temptation to use the 'spare' time to daydream

- labelling – putting somebody into a category before hearing what they have to say

- counselling – being unable to resist interrupting and giving advice

- duelling – countering the other's advances with thrusts of your own, e.g. 'Well at least this department is never over budget'

- side-stepping sentiment – countering expressions of emotion with jokes or hollow clichés, such as 'Well it's not the end of the world'.

There are also health factors that may cause difficulties in concentrating on what is being said. People who are suffering from stress, who are in pain or are anxious about something will not be at their best when it comes to effective communications.

If you are to do your job properly then it is important that you listen carefully to all instructions, help and advice.

6 Teams

6.1 Introduction

A work team can be a department, section or group with a set of common tasks. It is a part of a larger organisation with one person in charge of it, although every member of the team has some input into the way it operates.

Teams are groups of people who show the following characteristics:

- They share a common goal, and are striving to get a common job done.

- They enjoy working together, and enjoy helping one another.

- They have made a commitment to achieve the goals and objectives of the project by accomplishing their particular portion of the project.

- They are very diverse individuals having all kinds of different disciplinary and experiential backgrounds who must now concentrate on a common effort.

- They have great loyalty to the project as well as loyalty and respect for the project manager, and have a firm belief in what the project is trying to accomplish.

- They have attained a team spirit and very high team morale.

6.2 Team performance

An important aspect of work is that it is usually done in groups or teams. It does not matter whether the work is developing a corporate strategy for an organisation, checking insurance claims in an office or building cars in a factory. A team is quite simply a number of individuals working together to achieve a common task.

There are a number of factors that contribute to the performance of teams; for instance, the organisational structure within which the team works, the type of task to be accomplished, resources available and the characteristics of the team and the team members.

Many jobs within an organisation are impossible on an individual basis and take place as part of a team or a group. Although it is necessary to have such a group, for example a department such as the accounts department or a production group within the manufacturing area, it is also necessary to recognise that group relationships can be even more complex than individual relationships.

The main factors to take into consideration when working within a group or closely knit department are as follows:

- The varying members of the group are likely to have a wide variety of personalities. You will have to work closely, possibly even constantly, with this group of people and therefore must be prepared to put up with the various types of personality within the group.

- **Individual aptitudes and skills** – again it is likely that any team will be made up of a group of people with a variety of different aptitudes and skills. The group will require each of these aptitudes and skills and this should be remembered when dealing with other members of the group.

- **Goals** – it is likely that each work group will have particular goals or aims. If the goals or aims of the individual members of the group do not coincide with those of the group as a whole then there is likely to be conflict and pressures affecting members of the group. Wherever possible a student should try to tie in his/her own goals with those of the group. For example if the group concerned is the accounting department then provision of accurate and relevant information will be the group's goal and a student studying for AAT levels of competence should also have similar types of goals regarding accuracy and relevance.

- **Communication** – a group can only operate effectively if there is full communication at all levels and between all parties in the group. If you do work as part of a group then you should ensure that you understand exactly what the group is doing, why it is being done and what part you are required to play in this.

- **Deadlines** – deadlines in general have been considered earlier in the study text. In a group or team context you should be even more aware of the importance of deadlines. If you are asked to produce information or a piece of work by a particular time or date then if this deadline is not met it is likely to affect the workings of the entire group.

Organisations are increasingly becoming aware of the importance of teams working effectively, and how in doing so this can contribute to the organisation's success. One way of doing this is by considering how an existing group can be developed into a team. Some organisations use team-building courses to help with this process. The objective of team building is to improve the team's performance by:

- encouraging effective working practices

- reducing difficulties the team encounters

- improving work procedures

- improving interpersonal relationships between team members.

The benefits of team building are:

- it increases the chances of real improvement in performance because the whole team is involved

- it gives the team a chance to stop and think about the way the work is done.

6.3 Teamwork

There are very few jobs in which it is not necessary to work as part of a team.

Being part of a team means dealing with people at all levels within your organisation and building professional relationships with them. It takes time to build this association with people but there are a few guidelines, which might get you off to a good start:

(a) be tactful and courteous

(b) treat with respect people who are your senior in either age or position

(c) have a pleasant and helpful manner

(d) make allowances for others having personal problems which may affect their work, but do not joke about it or expect them to tell you why they might be having a 'bad day'

(e) communicate with people using the correct words and tone.

6.4 Commitments to others

It is firstly necessary to consider what a commitment actually is. 'A commitment is a firm agreement to do something within a particular time scale or at a particular time'.

A commitment is therefore binding, within a business context. The main reason for this is that the person to whom the commitment has been made has probably made corresponding commitments to other parties either within the organisation or outside of the organisation based upon your commitment.

We can also describe commitment as something that happens when team members see themselves as belonging to the team instead of as individuals acting on their own initiative. It is evident when the team members are committed to the team goals over and above their own personal goals.

6.5 Agreed time scales

In most organisations if you are required to produce information then the time scale for producing it will be discussed with you rather than simply being imposed. If you believe that the time scale proposed is unrealistic then you should say so, explaining why you hold this belief. You should never make promises that you cannot keep. The consequences of not producing work for a specified deadline are far worse than those of admitting that a deadline currently being set is unrealistic. It is far better to ensure that a reasonable deadline or time scale is set at the outset of the project rather than having to extend the deadline, or indeed not meet it, later in the project.

It is appreciated that it is sometimes difficult to speak up when dealing with those of a higher authority than yourself. However the final consequences should be borne in mind in all situations.

6.6 Personality differences

Having a professional relationship with someone is different from a social relationship. In a social relationship you can choose how well you get to know someone, even whether or not you get to know them in the first place.

At work you will inevitably have to deal with people whom you would not necessarily choose as friends. This does not mean that you have to treat them as friends, but as colleagues. This means being polite to other people and speaking to them in an appropriate tone of voice. It also means offering to help them if you can see they need help.

It can be difficult if you do have a personality clash with someone at any level, but you must keep it in proportion. One of the worst things you can do is to dwell on the problem. You will quickly become unpopular with your other colleagues if you talk continually about your problems with another member of staff. It may also mean that the other person hears about your complaints, which makes the matter worse.

6.7 Complaints

Staff morale is very important wherever you work and you can contribute to it. In the short term, everyone likes to complain about things, but in the long term this can cause tensions within the office.

In some cases, however, you may have a genuine cause for complaint. You should discreetly arrange to see your manager or personnel manager to discuss the problem. Remember that they will not necessarily have all the answers but will expect you to suggest solutions. Think carefully first about what you want to say and be positive.

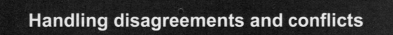

7 Handling disagreements and conflicts

7.1 Disagreements and conflicts

Although one would hope that the vast majority of work time would pass without disagreement between individuals or conflicts within a team there will be circumstances in which such disagreements or conflicts do occur. There is no avoiding such situations and students should think carefully about how to deal with them.

The general rule should be that if there is a disagreement or conflict with a fellow employee then this should be dealt with at a higher level of management rather than between the individual employees. There is little to be gained from two employees losing their tempers with each other if a manager can solve the problem or produce some sort of compromise.

A second important consideration is that it is usually far more constructive to recognise any conflict and discuss this with a manager rather than try to avoid or simply smooth over the problem.

There are likely to be simple personality conflicts between students and other employees, but these should be dealt with on a polite and professional basis. Any disagreement or conflict on a work matter should normally, however, be taken to a higher authority through the organisation's Grievance Procedure. Grievances can include unfair treatment by managers e.g. being passed over for promotion because of gender or race, unfair pay – men being paid more than women and unfair dismissal (an extreme case).

7.2   Managing disagreements and conflicts

There are many ways of managing conflict and disagreements and the suitability of any particular action will be determined by the situation. Several possible ways of resolving conflicts and disagreements are detailed below:

(i)   **Problem solving** – the individuals/team are brought together to find a solution to the particular problem.

(ii)   **Common goal** – finding a common goal that is more important than the differences of team members/individuals.

(iii)   **Allocating resources** – ending conflict over resources e.g. use of computers, by giving extra resources.

(iv)   **Compromise** – finding a solution without there being a defined winner or loser.

(v)   **Management decisions** – management making a decision.

(vi)   **Altering the team/individual's role** – changing team members and/or their roles.

To be successful in resolving conflicts and disagreements you must understand the reason for it, why the team/individual is behaving in such a way and what their expectations are.

KAPLAN PUBLISHING

7.3 Negotiation

Disagreements and negative conflict lead to:

- the misuse of resources, time, energy and creativity

- an increase in hostility

- a decrease in trust and openness

- a decrease in the ability of groups and the organisation as a whole to achieve the set objectives.

The best way of managing negative conflict is by negotiation, because the potential outcome is much more positive than with any other approach. The ultimate goal when resolving a conflict is for both parties to be satisfied with the outcome. Ideally, this means that both individuals get what they want. In reality, both individuals may have to compromise and get most of what they want, especially if their goals are mutually exclusive. This type of solution is called WIN-WIN because both individuals feel satisfied with the outcome, they both win. This type of solution involves a commitment by both parties to work out the problem fairly via compromise. However, there are times when this commitment is absent. When that happens, less ideal solutions are probable. These solutions may take the following forms:

WIN-LOSE – one party gets what it wants but the other does not.

LOSE-WIN – the first party does not get what it wants but the other does.

LOSE-LOSE – neither party gets what it wants.

Everyone negotiates – almost every day – and certain principles seem to be present which anyone can learn.

- **Ask questions** – before stating a position or making proposals, it is very helpful to inquire about the other side's interests and concerns. This will help you understand what is important to the other side and may provide new ideas for mutual benefit. Ask clarifying questions to really understand the other's concerns in this negotiation. This will also help you determine their approach to negotiations: win-lose or win-win. You can then make more realistic proposals.

- **'Win-win' negotiations** involve understanding each other's interests and finding solutions that will benefit both parties. The goal is to co-operate and seek solutions so both parties can walk away winners. If you come to the table thinking only one person can win (win-lose), there won't be an effort to co-operate or problem solve. By the same token, if you come to the table expecting to lose (lose-win), you play the martyr and resentment builds.

- **Respect** – when the other side feels that you respect him or her, it reduces defensiveness and increases the sharing of useful information, which can lead to an agreement. When people feel disrespect, they become more rigid and likely to hide information you need.

- **Trust** – people tend to be more generous toward those they like and trust. An attitude of friendliness and openness generally is more persuasive than an attitude of deception and manipulation. Being honest about the information you provide and showing interest in the other side's concerns can help.

7.4 The skills of a negotiator

The skills of a negotiator can be summarised under three main headings:

- **Interpersonal skills** – the use of good communicating techniques, the use of power and influence, and the ability to impress a personal style on the tactics of negotiation.

- **Analytical skills** – the ability to analyse information, diagnose problems, to plan and set objectives, and the exercise of good judgement in interpreting results.

- **Technical skills** – attention to detail and thorough case preparation.

In most situations a negotiation strategy is not an easy option but it is one that has much more of a positive outcome than an imposed solution. The first step is to get the parties to trust you. Next, you can try to find as much common ground as there is between the parties and encourage them to arrive at a middle ground. If neither party get what they want then you have a lose-lose situation. This is a very common situation where compromise comes in. Unfortunately, compromises result in needs not being satisfied. You are aiming for a win-win situation, where both parties get as close as possible to what they really want. This situation is not always possible but working towards it can achieve mutual respect, co-operation, enhanced communication and more creative problem solving. You need to start by identifying what both parties really want – as opposed to what they think they want. The parties also need to explain what they want it for and what will happen if they do not get it. This procedure is a severe test of a manager's interpersonal skills, but it could bring about the best solution.

7.5   Negotiating styles

Negotiating styles that can be used are competing, collaborating, compromising, accommodating, and avoiding.

Competing – 'hard bargaining' or 'might makes right'

Pursuing personal concerns at the expense of the other party. Competing can mean 'standing up for your rights' defending a position that you believe is correct or simply trying to win.

Collaborating – 'sharing tasks and responsibilities' or 'two heads are better than one'

Working with someone by exploring your disagreement, generating alternatives, and finding a solution that mutually satisfies the concerns of both parties.

Compromising – 'splitting the difference'

Seeking a middle ground by 'splitting the difference', the solution that satisfies both parties.

Accommodating – 'soft bargaining' or 'killing your enemy with kindness'

Yielding to another person's point of view – paying attention to their concerns and neglecting your own.

Avoiding – 'leave well enough alone'

Not addressing the conflict, either by withdrawing from the situation or postponing the issues.

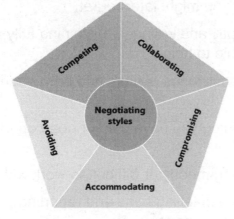

Activity 2

You work in quite a large accounts department. Your manager has three deputies and the rule is that only one of them can be away on holiday or attend a course at a time. All three approach him in March asking for the same two weeks off in June. Tom, who is the most senior of the three, wants to do a sponsored bike ride in Cuba. Dick wants to take his family to Las Vegas for his brother's wedding. Harry has been accepted on a special course that will enhance his promotional prospects.

Each of them hears about the other's applications and they have a furious row and now only talk to each other about work-related matters.

Outline five different ways the manager can deal with this situation.

7.6   Maintaining good relationships

Once you have created a good relationship with other staff, this must be maintained because it is important for the following reasons:

(a)   staff who are happy and co-operate with each other work harder and are more productive

(b)   morale and motivation are improved.

Be the ideal member of staff that everyone appreciates by:

(a)   communicating with people in a mature and professional manner

(b)   thinking through the consequence of your words and actions before you say or do anything that you might later regret

(c)   carrying out requests promptly and willingly, explaining fully and politely when you are not able to help

(d)   asking others for help and assistance politely and only when necessary

(e)   informing others about anything you have said or done on their behalf

(f)   bearing no grudges, not being moody or difficult to work with

(g)   knowing the difference between telling tales and reporting unethical behaviour or problems to your superior

(h)   finding solutions for any conflicts and dissatisfaction that could reduce personal effectiveness and team effectiveness.

8 Summary

This chapter has demonstrated the need to be sensitive to the responsibilities and commitments of your colleagues' workloads. It has also described how communication between individuals and within teams can be improved and how communication can be altered according to the goals and context of the situation. You should now understand how empathy and sensitivity to the needs, background and position of colleagues (both more junior and more senior) will improve professionalism and performance of the whole organisation and how this can help to establish constructive working relationships.

Answers to chapter activities

Activity 1

Scenario 1

The quotations manager is currently in a meeting with a prospective customer. He is presenting a quotation to that customer for a series of contracts; however the price is based upon the existing price of XX5, which is £2.65 per kg.

If this information does not reach the quotation manager during this meeting there is a possibility that the prospective customer will be lost to a competitor, as the price quoted will not be low enough.

Scenario 2

The quotations manager is currently in his office making a number of telephone calls. He is in fact telephoning a variety of alternative suppliers in order to find a lower price than the current £2.65 per kg for XX5.

If this information does not reach the quotations manager promptly then he may agree a price higher than £2.42 with an alternative supplier.

Scenario 3

The quotations manager is just about to enter a meeting with the production manager. At that meeting they will discuss the use of an alternative product to XX5 that can be purchased at a price cheaper than the current £2.65 per kg of XX5. It is suspected that the product is of inferior quality to XX5 but the needs of cost cutting are too great to ignore.

If the information regarding the reduced price of XX5 does not reach the quotations manager then there is a possibility that future production may use an inferior product, which can be purchased at a price cheaper than the current £2.65 per kg.

Activity 2

Your manager you could deal with the situation in the following ways.

- Call them all together and explain they must sort the matter out themselves but, if they fail to do so, you will sort the matter out for them by exercising your right to determine the holiday rota, and that no one will be allowed to go that fortnight anyway. If you go for this option, you are choosing the power route. This is fine if jobs are scarce, but highly risky. If you win, they all lose!

- Call them all together and tell them they must sort the matter out themselves. By choosing this option and letting them sort it out themselves you are avoiding the situation.

- Talk the matter over with each of them separately to discuss the facts with them. Make a decision as to whose need is the most pressing, then get them all together and announce your decision. This option is an attempt at a compromise, although not allowing very much input from them.

- Tell them individually not to be silly, and suggest they take an afternoon off and talk the matter over with their families/friends/training officer. This solution of patting them on the head and telling them to talk to others is trying to defuse the situation.

- Discuss all the problems the situation raises with each fully and, if the matter still cannot be sorted out, go to the training officer and see if there is an alternative course; and the Chief Officer to see if on this occasion two deputies can be allowed on holiday at the same time. Bring them all back to hear the outcome. Only this option begins to address the problems. Even though there is no knowing there will be a successful outcome, you are trying to resolve all the conflicting needs.

A team-building approach can promote openness and discussion of problems like these, meaning that there will be fewer destructive conflicts to cope with.

Improving your own performance

7

Introduction

The appraisal of performance should identify your strengths and weaknesses and this can be the starting point for a career plan. Your strategy will then be designed to use your strengths and overcome any weaknesses so that you can take advantage of career opportunities.

A competence is an observable skill or ability to complete a particular task. It also includes the ability to transfer skills and knowledge to a new situation. The general purpose of any assessment or appraisal is to improve the efficiency of the organisation by ensuring that the individual employees are performing to the best of their ability and developing their potential for improvement.

KNOWLEDGE	CONTENTS
1.3 Identify appropriate working lines within your organisation.	1 Identify your own development needs
4.1 Explain the importance of continuing professional development and identify your own development needs and objectives.	2 Career planning
	3 Process of competence assessment
	4 Learning to improve your importance
4.2 Monitor and review your own development needs and objectives.	5 Methods used to acquire skills and knowledge
	6 Review and evaluate your performance and progress

1 Identify your own development needs

1.1 Becoming an accounting technician

There are many reasons to become an accounting technician. If you think you deserve a better career with improved prospects and a higher earning potential, then becoming an accounting technician is an ideal first step to achieving these goals and more.

You will be qualified to work in any number of accounting roles, in a wide range of industries – you do not have to work for an accounting firm.

As an AAT qualified accounting technician you will have an internationally recognised and respected qualification that shows potential employers that you have been trained to a high standard.

In addition, as the AAT's qualification is founded on actually doing the work, they will know that as well as the underpinning knowledge, you have the skills and practical experience not just to perform in an accounting role, but also to excel in it.

And if you are thinking of training to be a chartered or certified accountant then the AAT is an ideal route to these qualifications. All the main UK CA bodies offer exemptions to AAT qualified members.

1.2 What is development?

Development is the growth or realisation of a person's ability and potential through the provision of learning and educational experiences.

Organisations often have a training and development strategy based on the overall strategy for the business.

Development activities include:

- career planning
- training – both on and off the job
- appraisal
- other learning opportunities e.g. job rotation.

Training can be described as the planned and systematic modification of behaviour through learning events, programmes and instruction which enable individuals to achieve the level of knowledge, skills and competence to carry out their work effectively.

All training and development is self-development, whether it is provided by the organisation or not. If you do not want to learn, acquire new skills, change attitudes or behaviour or are not sufficiently motivated to do so, you will not manage it. If the outcome of an appraisal programme or promotion planning incorporates training that is imposed it cannot lead to effective development.

Some organisations make a commitment to individual development, which requires the setting of individual objectives and the negotiation of a learning contract between the organisation and the employee. It allows the individual to select the way in which learning will take place, the provision of support and guidance by the organisation and joint assessment of the results.

1.3   Development opportunities

Your manager should be able to refer you to others who can assist you in achieving your development and suggest appropriate referral sources both within and outside the department e.g. books, journals, professional associations or people who might be willing to serve as mentors.

You can do your own research into developments relating to your job and also relating to the AAT and where it will lead you.

Make a note of useful addresses and look out for publications that keep you up-to-date with developments relating to your job role.

Association of Accounting Technicians

140 Aldersgate Street,
London EC1A 4HY

Tel: +44 (0)20 7397 3000

Fax: +44 (0)20 7397 3009

Website: www.aat.org.uk

The AAT – ACA fast track is a direct route to qualification as a Chartered Accountant – from the AAT.

For the first two years of the Fast Track, you train for the AAT as normal, making sure you have completed certain units and kept a record of your work experience. After that, if you obtain an ACA training contract and pass a Top Up paper, you effectively bypass the first year of training, leaving you just two years away from a top financial business qualification.

The Institute of Chartered Accountants in England & Wales

Chartered Accountants' Hall
PO Box 433
London EC2P 2BJ

Tel 020 7920 8100

Fax 020 7920 0547

There are many on-line resources that will give you more information:
AAT – www.accountingtechnician.co.uk

Financial Times Self-Assessment –
http://ftcareerpoint.ft.com/YourCareer/developyourself

Financial Times – Mastering Management – www.ftmastering.com

Financial Times – Business Education – www.ft.com/surveys/businessed

Your People Manager – www.yourpeoplemanager.com

Many colleges will run courses that you might consider. They also have
websites, or will send you brochures, which you might find interesting.

2 Career planning

2.1 Why plan?

Today emphasis is on lifelong learning and multiple job/career transitions.
The aim of career development is to help you understand your potential
and to help you maximise this potential in the work force today and in the
future. From the start, you will need to have a clear idea of the kind of
career path you would like to follow. Good career planning can lead to a
satisfying career. People who do not career plan usually get sick from
stress working in fields they do not like, and students waste time and
money pursuing educational areas in which they have no interest. The
decisions we make about careers and leisure activities throughout our life
span are critical to our sense of well being. Satisfaction in our work can be
a key ingredient to our feelings of self-worth. Happiness can be contingent
upon a role as productive and worthwhile employer or employee.
Conversely, excessive stress on the job can interfere with our health and
personal relationships. Many believe that a person who balances work
with life roles find fulfilment in the work place as well as in his or her other
life roles as citizen, student, parent, etc. When planning your future you
need to understand that career development is often a lifetime project and
may require continuous learning.

2.2 Preparing a SWOT analysis

One of the most difficult tasks is to gain insight into yourself – your
strengths and weaknesses – yet this is an essential first step in developing
a career plan. You need to know whether you are an introvert or an
extrovert and whether you have the right approach towards achievement,
work, material things, time and change. Different personal skills are
required for interacting with other people, goal planning, self-development,

motivation and performance. Many firms evaluate people on such personality factors as aggressiveness, co-operation, leadership and attitude.

Capabilities or skills may be categorised as:

- **technical** – involves working with tools and specific techniques

- **human** – the ability to work with people; it is co-operative effort; it is teamwork and the creation of an environment in which people feel secure and free to express their opinions

- **conceptual skill** – is the ability to see the 'big picture', to recognise significant elements in a situation and to understand the relationships among the elements

- **design skill** – is the ability to solve problems in ways that will benefit the organisation.

The relative importance of these skills differs for the various positions in the organisational hierarchy, with technical skills being very important at the supervisory level, conceptual skills being crucial for top managers and human skills being important for all positions.

It is also important to make a careful assessment of the external environment, including its opportunities and threats. For example, joining an expanding company usually provides more career opportunities than working for a mature company that is not expected to grow.

E-learning might make it easier for some people to achieve their qualifications than attending classes at colleges etc.

Strengths	Weaknesses
– What are your advantages? (colleagues will identify these)	– What could be improved? (assessment by supervisor will identify any weaknesses)
– What do you do well? (competence analysis will identify strengths and development needs)	– What is done badly?
	– What should you avoid?

Opportunities	Threats
– What are the interesting trends? (keep up-to-date with courses, colleagues and managers as well as publications)	– What obstacles do you face?
	– Is changing technology threatening your position?
– Does your organisation have high turnover of managerial staff? (appraisals will outline the range of opportunities)	– Is your job changing?

2.3　Career strategy

The most successful strategy would be to build on your strengths and take advantage of opportunities. For example, if you have an excellent knowledge of computing and many organisations are looking for accountants who are also computer literate, you should find many opportunities for a satisfying career. On the other hand, if there is a demand for accountants with computing skills and you are interested but lack the necessary skills, the proper approach would be to develop the skills so that you can take advantage of the opportunities.

People do not always choose the most obvious career because it might not be the most fulfilling one. The choice involves personal preferences, ambitions and values. For example, although you might have certain computing skills demanded in the job market, that type of job may not interest you and it might be preferable to broaden your knowledge and skills or deal more with people.

You must also consider whether your choice is realistic and achievable in terms of resources and support from relevant people. You may be thinking of undertaking this entirely on a distance-learning basis or you may need to attend college on a day release or full time basis. You may be receiving support from your organisation for this in terms of money and time or you may be entirely self-financing. The qualification may just be one element in a complex and highly structured development programme. Some accountancy career paths take a long time, are quite expensive and require a lot of spare time to be devoted to study. If you have a family to consider, this must be discussed thoroughly before you broach the subject at work. An effective career strategy requires that consideration be given to the career of your spouse. Dual career couples sometimes have to make very stressful choices, especially when it comes to opportunities for promotion that require relocation.

Even without a family there might be constraints in terms of personal relationships that would suffer if you did not give them your full attention.

Career choices require trade-offs. Some alternatives involve high risks, others low risk. Some choices demand action now; other choices can wait. Your plans are developed in an environment of uncertainty and the future cannot be predicted with great accuracy. Therefore, contingency plans based on alternative assumptions should also be prepared. For example, while you might enjoy working for a fast-growing venture company, it might be wise to prepare an alternative career plan based on the assumption that the venture might not succeed.

KAPLAN PUBLISHING

2.4 Growth

Your objective should be to ensure 'growth' during your career. This objective can obviously benefit your organisation as well as you. The growth should be triggered by a job that provides challenging, stretching goals. The clearer and more challenging the goals, the more effort you will exert, and the more likely it is that good performance will result. If you do a good job and receive positive feedback, you will feel successful (psychological success). These feelings will increase your feelings of confidence and self-esteem. This should lead to you becoming more involved in your work, which in turn leads to the setting of future stretching goals. This career-growth cycle is outlined below:

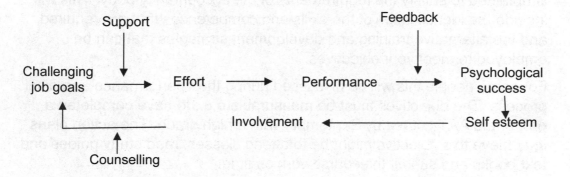

The above cycle can only be successfully completed if you receive support from your supervisor or manager.

2.5 Development goals/objectives

Once the direction of your career has been identified, the strategy has to be supported by objectives and action plans.

Short-term goals should be attainable within one year; medium-term goals within three years; and long-term goals within five years. Each goal should have a specific target and the deadlines by which these targets should be achieved should be stated, although flexibility should be retained to allow for unforeseen circumstances.

Your goals and objectives will be aimed at:

- performance in the current job
- future changes in the current role
- moving elsewhere within the organisation · developing specialist expertise.

Your manager can support your career development by informing you about options for improvement and possible barriers to career movement, encouraging you to focus on clear, specific and attainable career goals or suggesting steps you might take to improve existing skills and knowledge.

Some organisations make a commitment to individual development, which requires the setting of individual objectives and the negotiation of a learning contract between you and the organisation. It allows you to select the way in which learning will take place, the provision of support and guidance by the organisation and joint assessment of the results.

If you are seeking membership of one of the accountancy bodies the selection of the most appropriate qualification and methods of study will have to be determined by discussions between you, the accountant and the training officer (this may have been agreed at the selection interview). In addition a training programme must be initiated so that the correct practical experience

is obtained to satisfy the requirements of the accountancy body. This will include the identification of the skills and competences that are required and the alternative training and development strategies that can be employed to meet your objectives.

For some people this will be discussed during their performance appraisal process. The objectives must be measurable e.g., to have completed a part of the AAT course by September with a high grade. The action plans to achieve this objective might be to attend classes, read study guides and text books and submit the coursework on time.

2.6   Monitoring progress

Monitoring is the process of evaluating your progress towards career goals and making necessary corrections to the aims or plans. Having embarked on your career path you must demonstrate effective time-management and efficient task-achievement so that you can accomplish your objectives in the time you have allowed yourself.

As well as self-monitoring, you will hopefully be receiving help, encouragement and feedback from your supervisor or manager. During your performance appraisal, your progress will be discussed and you will be encouraged to review your performance against objectives in the operating areas of your job and also to review the achievement of milestones in your career path.

3 Process of competence assessment

3.1 Competencies

A competence is an observable ability to complete a specific task successfully. Competencies are the critical skills, knowledge and attitude that a jobholder must have to perform effectively. There are three different types of competence:

- behavioural competences include the ability to relate well to others

- occupational competences cover what people have to do to achieve the results in the job

- generic competences that apply to anyone, e.g. adaptability, initiative.

They are expressed in visible, behavioural terms and reflect the skills, knowledge and attitude (the main components of any job) which must be demonstrated to an agreed standard and must contribute to the overall aims of the organisation.

The term is open to various interpretations because there are a number of competence-based systems and concepts of competence. As a general definition, a competent individual can perform a work role in a wide range of settings over an extended period of time.

Some competence-based systems are achievement-led – they focus on assessment of competent performance – what people do at work and how well they do it. Others are development-led – they focus on the development of competence and are linked to training and development programmes to develop people to a level of performance expected at work. Actual training needs may be categorised on the basis of the following competencies:

Work quality:

- technical and task knowledge

- accuracy and consistency

- exercise of judgement and discretion

- communication skills

- cost consciousness.

Work quantity:

- personal planning and time management
- capacity to meet deadlines or work under pressure
- capacity to cope with upward variations in work volume.

Supervisory and managerial skills and competencies:

- planning and organising
- communication and interpersonal skills
- directing, guiding and motivating
- leadership and delegation
- co-ordination and control
- developing and retaining staff
- developing teamwork.

3.2 Process

Competences are defined by means of a competence (or capability, or functional) analysis. This process describes:

- the job's main tasks or key result areas
- the types and levels of knowledge and skill that these require
- the acceptable standard of performance in each task or result area ·
  how performance is assessed.

Installing a competence-based system means:

- establishing the elements of competence – activity, skill or ability required by the job holder to perform the job
- establishing the criteria of performance of the skill or ability required and setting standards to measure it by
- measuring the actual performance against the standard
- taking corrective action where there is any deviation from the standard.

The control element of the system allows feedback to change the elements of competence or the criteria of measurement in the light of actions taken and feedback given by the job-holder.

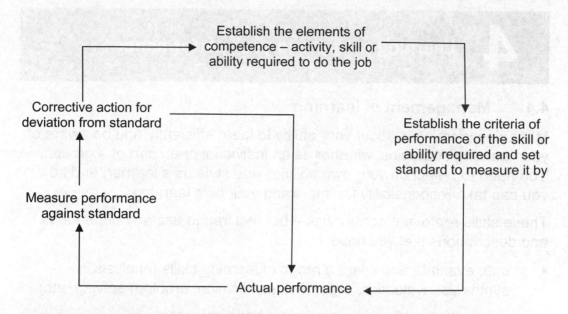

Although it is not a work-based activity, think of the process of passing a driving test. It is an observable skill that is measured against set standards. In the case of failure a list that outlines the failed areas is given to the learner driver and is used to form the basis of any corrective action needed before re-applying for the test.

The Lead Body guidelines for the AAT units that make up your course, are written as statements incorporating:

- elements of competence – specific activities a job holder should be able to perform

- performance criteria – how well it should be performed

- a range statement – in what context and conditions

- the knowledge and understanding that underpins the competence.

📝 Activity 1

After studying this section you should be able to explain the process of competence assessment.

---

4 Learning to improve your performance

4.1 Management of learning

Managing learning is about your ability to learn efficiently and be aware of your learning strategies, whether as an individual or as part of a group. You need to reflect on your own abilities and style as a learner, and how you can take responsibility for improving your own learning.

These skills represent possibilities – but feel free to use any other ideas and descriptions that you have:

- use, evaluate and adapt a range of learning skills (analysis, synthesis, evaluation, argument, justification, problem-solving, etc)
- purposefully reflect on own learning and progress
- demonstrate awareness of learning processes
- use learning in new or different situations/contexts
- assist/support others in learning and learn from peers
- develop, evaluate and adapt learning strategies
- carry out agreed tasks
- work productively in a co-operative context
- learn through collaboration
- provide constructive feedback to colleagues
- assist/support others in learning
- interact effectively with supervisor/wider group
- develop business awareness
- evaluate own potential for employment.

4.2 Self-management

Self-management is about your personal organisational skills and being able to cope with the demands of managing your work, your studying, your college life, and beyond. It might also include addressing your personal values and commitments. You need to ask yourself, whether you:

- manage time effectively
- set realistic objectives, priorities and standards
- listen actively and with purpose
- show intellectual flexibility and creativity

- take responsibility for acting in a professional/ethical manner

- plan/work towards long-term aims and goals

- purposely reflect on own learning and progress

- take responsibility for own learning/personal growth

- demonstrate awareness of learning processes

- clarify personal values

- cope with physical demands/stress

- monitor, evaluate and adapt own performance.

4.3 Communication skills

Communication obviously underpins all aspects of life. At work it will often be oral but written and visual communication is equally important. How good are you at expressing ideas and opinions, at speaking or writing with confidence and clarity, at presenting yourself to a variety of audiences? You should be able to:

- use appropriate language and form in a range of activities (reports, presentations, interviews, etc)

- present information/ideas competently (oral, written, visual)

- respond to different purposes/contexts/audiences

- persuade rationally by means of appropriate information

- defend/justify views or actions

- take initiative and lead others

- negotiate with individuals/the group

- offer constructive criticism

- listen actively and effectively

- evaluate and adapt strategies for communication.

4.4 Team/group work/management of others

Do you fit well into a team? Are you a leader? Have you had a wide experience of working with different types of group, whether formal or informal? Have you been on a team development course? Do you work in study groups, or project groups, or manage meetings for a club or society? Consider your skills of co-operation, delegation or negotiation. How have you worked and learned with others?

The following skills would indicate your group working abilities:

- carry out agreed tasks
- respect the views and values of others
- work productively in a co-operative context
- adapt to the needs of the group/team
- defend/justify views or actions
- take initiative and lead others
- delegate and stand back
- offer constructive criticism
- take the role of chairperson
- learn through collaboration
- negotiate with individuals/the group
- assist/support others in learning from peers
- interact effectively with tutor/wider group
- monitor, evaluate and assess processes of group/team work.

4.5 Problem-solving

Do you like tackling and solving problems? How do you manage your job tasks? Can you identify the main features of a problem and develop strategies for its resolution? Are you able to monitor your performance and improve on strategies? Some subjects may traditionally be perceived as related to problem-solving (say, computing), but, for most of us, in any subject area, assignments such as reports or presentations present us with a variety of problems to be solved.

Problem-solving skills means you need to be able to:

- identify key features of the problem/task
- conceptualise issues
- identify strategic options
- plan and implement a course of action
- organise sub-tasks
- set and maintain priorities
- think laterally about a problem
- apply theory to practical context
- apply knowledge/tools/methods to solution of problems

- manage physical resources (tools/equipment)

- show confidence in responding creatively to problems

- show awareness of issues of health and safety

- monitor, evaluate and adapt strategies and outcomes.

5 Methods used to acquire skills and knowledge

5.1 Personal development plan (PDP)
Continuing Professional Development (CPD)

CPD is defined as the systematic maintenance enhancement and continuous improvement of knowledge skills and ability oftem term competence, that one needs to work professionally as an accounting technician.

Your CPD needs are thus expressed in terms of an personal development plan (PDP)

Basically there are four main options you should consider for each of the development needs within your PDP:

- **Education** – this option will most likely lead to a qualification and will provide you with a broad based body of knowledge, which in turn you need to be able to apply in the work place. With the introduction of more flexible delivery methods you can mix and match between taught modules, self-study and open learning and an increasing availability of e-learning facilities.

- **Training** – this option will be most useful when you need to focus on a particular skill or skill set and can be delivered in many ways: in house, off the job, on the job, by instructors or trainers, or by self-learning.

- **Development** – this option is a combination of all the other options and should be planned with clear learning goals and measurable outcomes. Ideally the PDP will be aligned with the organisations objectives and your career aspirations.

- **Experience** – we know that there is no substitute for experience, but we also know that many experiences can be painful. Throwing someone in at the deep end may work for some but it is a lot safer if the person doing the throwing knows how deep it is and is on the sideline if difficulties arise. Setting stretching goals and objectives and having coaching and mentoring support will provide a really powerful way of growing and developing yourself.

5.2   Training solutions

A training needs analysis addresses the following:

- What skills does my organisation need me to have to perform my current tasks effectively?

- What skills do I need to ensure are maintained?

- What aspects of my work do I enjoy and wish to develop?

- What personal qualities do I need to enhance?

- What training resources are available to me?

- What learning methods suit me best?

- Where do I expect to be in five years' time?

The training plan is constructed from an investigation into training needs and includes the identification of the skills and knowledge required by the labour force, the identification of the skills and knowledge already possessed – the difference between the two providing a picture of the job-centred training needs. This is then incorporated into the organisation's training plan and decisions are taken on priorities, location, duration, timing and content of training.

Training objectives should be specific and related to observable targets that can be measured. They will cover:

- **behaviour** – what you should be able to do

- **standard** – the level of performance

- **environment** – the conditions.

Once the training objectives are identified, the training funds available and the priorities established in relation to the urgency of the training, the training decisions must be made. These include decisions on the scale and type of training system needed, and whether it can best be provided by the organisation's own staff or by external consultants. Training methods, timing and duration, location and the people actually doing the training also needs to be decided.

Training may be carried out 'in-house' or externally. If any of the training is done in-house, decisions will need to be made on such things as:

- training workshops

- location and equipping of classrooms

- selection of training officers.

Colleges, universities, training organisations and management consultants may provide external courses. There are also open and distance learning facilities via the Open University and other programmes.

To make sure that the training needs are being met, separate training and development co-ordinators may be allocated the responsibilities for training within the firm and for any external training. They may also be responsible for reviewing the system on a regular basis to ensure that it is still satisfying those needs.

5.3 Researching training and development methods

Training and development methods vary tremendously depending on the person, the job, the resources, the organisation and the economic environment. You can divide them into on-the-job and off-the-job training methods, structured or unstructured, participatory or self development, sitting in front of a computer screen or 'sitting with Nellie'. The methods that you might be looking at include: training courses, both external and in-house; on-the-job training; mentoring; coaching; computerised interactive learning; planned experiences; and self-managed learning.

Business games, either in the sophisticated format of the computer based profit-seeking program or as the simple leadership games centred around packs of playing cards, are also effective tools of management development. The list of games available is endless; all involve high participation levels.

5.4 Internal training and development methods

You can research the types of training and development that can take place at work. These include:

- **Job instructions** – are a systematic approach to training for a particular job, normally used by supervisors when training those who report to them. It can be a cost-effective way of satisfying training needs and can also be linked to a competence-based qualification such as NVQ, which is supervised by the trainee's immediate superior.

- Internal training centres are sometimes used to provide customised training programmes e.g. where there would be a risk if the trainee made a mistake.

- **Job rotation** – the training idea of moving an employee from one job to another is that it broadens experience and encourages the employee to be aware of the total activity.

- **Films and closed circuit television** (CCTV) – Films are used to describe company situations, how the different functions of an organisation relate to one another, or for presenting an overview of production. CCTV is used increasingly in management training to illustrate how managers behave and to show how such behaviour can be modified to enable beneficial changes in their interpersonal and problem solving skills.

- **Computer-based training** (CBT) and computer assisted learning (CAL) – user-friendly systems enable trainees to work at their own pace, working on set programmes.

- **Programmed learning** – consists of the presentation of instructional material in small units followed immediately by a list of questions the trainee must answer correctly before progressing to more difficult work.

- **Coaching** – is a specialised form of communication with support being given from the planning stage and continuing during the learning process, with the value of constructive criticism being particularly relevant.

- **Mentoring** – the mentor is expected to guide the new recruit through a development programme and 'socialise' them into the culture of the enterprise. It is a route for bringing on 'high flyers' by allowing them to make mistakes under supervision.

- **Secondments** are temporary transfers to another department or division to gain a deeper understanding or learn more about certain aspects within an organisation.

- **Work shadowing** is a method where one employee shadows another, often more senior, to experience what it is like working at that level.

Activity 2

What type of training is most suitable for the following people?

- Senior lecturer in a university
- The son of the managing director taking over his father's business in the family firm
- New recruit into the payroll section of the account department
- Bank clerk needing to brush up on selling techniques

5.5   Internal training and development methods for groups

Group training encourages participants to learn from each other through discussing issues, pooling experiences and critically examining opposite viewpoints. Instructors guide discussions rather than impart knowledge directly. They monitor trainee's understanding of what is going on, ask questions to clarify points and sometimes, but not always, prevent certain members from dominating the group. Some of the most popular methods follow:

1   **The lecture method** – is an economical way of passing information to many people. Lectures are of little value if the aim of training is to change attitudes, or develop job or interpersonal skills.

2   **Discussion methods** – are known ways of securing interest and commitment. They can shape attitudes, encourage motivation and secure understanding and can also underline the difficulties of group problem solving.

3   **Case study method** – learning occurs through participation in the definition, analysis and solution of the problem or problems. It demonstrates the nature of group problem solving activity and usually underlines the view that there is no one best solution to a complex business problem.

4   **Role playing** – This method requires trainees to project themselves into a simulated situation that is intended to represent some relevant reality, say, a confrontation between management and a trade union. The merit of role-playing is that it influences attitudes, develops interpersonal skills and heightens sensitivity to the views and feelings of others.

5   **Business games** – simulate realistic situations, mergers, take-overs, etc in which groups compete with one another and where the effects of the decision taken by one group may affect others.

6   **T-group exercises** (the T stands for training) leave the group to their own devices. The trainer simply tells them to look after themselves and remains as an observer. The group itself have to decide what to do and, understandably, the members feel helpless at first and then they pool their experiences and help each other. They eventually form a cohesive group, appoint a leader and resolve any conflicts within the group. They exercise interpersonal communication skills and learn to understand group dynamics.

5.6   Self development

Self-development is taking personal responsibility for your own learning. This is an ongoing process that takes place wherever you are and that will continue throughout your life.

A very rich ground for learning, however, is in the workplace. You can have significant learning experiences by doing, being thrown in at the deep end, undertaking challenging new projects and even making mistakes! You can:

- learn ways to improve what you do now

- learn new skills to meet the changing needs of your employer or · prepare to move on to a new job.

Effective self-development means you need to focus on the following:

- Assess your current skills and interest through paper-and-pencil career tests or through computer programs that analyse skills and interests.

- Maintain a learning log or diary to help you analyse what you are learning from work experiences.

- Develop a personal development plan that identifies your learning needs and goals.

- Consciously seek out learning opportunities to meet your goals e.g. by watching colleagues and asking relevant questions.

- Actively seek feedback on performance/abilities/actions.

- Find a mentor who can provide you with support, advice, and assistance in your career direction.

- Become involved in professional organisations.

- Be opportunistic – look for learning opportunities outside of formal activities e.g. home, social, voluntary, etc.

- Read books, professional journals and trade magazines to keep current on the latest developments in your field.

- Use the Internet to browse for interesting sites and different views on subjects that interest you.

6 Review and evaluate your performance and progress

6.1 Assessment

In all organisations someone assesses the performance of each employee. Often this is a casual, subjective and infrequent activity where the manager or supervisor spontaneously mentions that a piece of work was done poorly or well. The subordinate then responds in an appropriate manner. It encourages desirable performance and discourages undesirable performance before it becomes ingrained. But increasingly, many organisations (particularly larger ones) have decided to formalise the assessment process and use it to improve performance, assess training needs and predict the potential of employees.

If you are studying for the AAT qualification you are assessed on your standards of competence; the focus being on what you have achieved – can you do what is being assessed? There are only three possible outcomes of an assessment:

- pass
- not yet competent
- insufficient evidence upon which to make a judgement.

The majority of the assessment is done at work and when you are ready for it. Assessment methods at NVQ level 3 may be practical, written and oral:

- **practical** – from observing performance within an organisation or department
- **written** – from examining entries in log books
- **oral** – from assessment of oral presentations or observation of leading discussions.

This method of assessment allows you to gain the level of competence required for your jobs in stages. The successful completion of a unit is recorded in the National Record of Achievement.

6.2 Appraisal

Performance appraisal is a formal procedure to ensure that employees receive objective feedback on their performance, in the context of organisational goals and enabling them to improve themselves. It is often used:

- to audit an employee's competences

- to identify potential and agree targets · to review achievements

- to communicate and align plans and priorities, both personal and the organisation's

- to identify training and development needs, and monitor career progression

- to exchange feedback and motivate an employee.

- A modern approach to setting goals and objectives for an employee is the application of SMART technique.

    The acronym SMART relates to the characteristics of sound objectives in that they should be:

    SPECIFIC

    MEASUREABLE

    ACHIEVABLE

    RELEVANT and;

    TIME BOUNDED

    When agreeing objectives set by your manager ensure that they meet all the elements listed above.

6.3 Techniques of appraisal

Appraisal techniques include the following:

- **Employee ranking** – Employees are ranked on the basis of their overall performance. This method is particularly prone to bias and its feedback value is practically zero. It does, however, have the advantage that it is simple to use.

- **Rating scales** – Graphic rating scales consist of general personal characteristics and personality traits such as quantity of work, initiative, co-operation and judgement. The judges rate the employee on a scale whose ratings vary, for example from low to high or from poor to excellent. It is called 'graphic' because the scale visually graphs performance from one extreme to the other.

- **Description/Report** – This is a qualitative method of assessment where the manager writes a brief description of the employee under a number of headings.

6.4 Self-appraisal

Self-appraisal is assessing your own capabilities and personal characteristics. Occupational Standards and Key/Core Skills provide a framework and language to describe them.

It is a vital component in managing your own professional development and will help you:

- plan and manage your career

- improve your job performance

- improve your capacity to learn

- increase your self confidence and present yourself more effectively

- identify and take advantage of job and learning opportunities

- obtain support from mentors and managers

- manage and provide support to others.

With a realistic self-appraisal you are more likely to be loyal to a supportive environment and committed to improving your own and colleagues' performance. It will enable you to develop yourself to your full potential, reliably managing your work and career. You are also more likely to make use of your training, development and experience as lifelong learning and provide good role models to others.

Steps to self-appraisal:

1   **Clarify personal aims** – focus on your objectives – how much is your self-appraisal for: improved work performance, enhanced career development or personal growth? Record your aims.

2   **Manage the appraisal** – find sources of help. Use the professional guidelines to identify relevant standards and key/core skills. Gather insights from others inside and outside the organisation according to personal circumstances. Record the results.

3   **Review personal experience** – look at CV, performance appraisal records, portfolios of evidence, and significant events. Assess values, interests, competences, motivation and contacts. Know yourself.

4 **Assess your own competencies** – assess yourself against occupational standards and key/core skills. Identify strengths, weaknesses, opportunities and threats. Analyse your job. Use diagnostic tools. Identify your priority competences in terms of relative importance of career competence needs and ease of access/opportunities for achieving.

5 **Assess what helps and hinders your development** – identify your learning style and forces for/against personal change.

6 **Review self-appraisal process** – identify the benefits. Record the results and improve the process.

7 Summary

This chapter has looked at ways of improving your own performance at work. Now that you have studied this chapter you should be able to identify your development needs and research appropriate ways of acquiring skills and knowledge. Training and development need to be reviewed from time to time, just as any other procedures. Some organisations have continuous assessment of training in general; others will have annual appraisals to monitor performance and review achievements.

KAPLAN PUBLISHING

Answers to chapter activities

Activity 1

Your explanation should include the fact that it is a way of measuring what people do at work and how well they do it.

After analysing a job, there should be a statement drawn up by the supervisor or manager establishing both the specific activities a jobholder should be able to perform and the performance criteria detailing how well it should be performed.

The assessment is predominantly by observation – the jobholder demonstrating how well he or she performs the activity. Feedback is given and assistance with corrective actions required where the performance does not match the standard set.

Activity 2

The type of training that is most suitable:

- Secondment might be considered for a senior lecturer in a university.

- Mentoring or coaching could be the best solution for the son of the managing director taking over his father's business in the family firm.

- Job instructions might be the quickest way to get the new recruit up to scratch on the payroll system.

- Programmed learning or computer-based training could give the bank clerk the ability to brush up on selling techniques.

WORKBOOK

KEY TECHNIQUES
QUESTIONS and ANSWERS

Key Techniques: Questions

3

Activity 1

What measures can an organisation take to reduce the risk of equipment being stolen?

Activity 2

Give examples of the type of fraud that might be perpetrated.

Activity 3

Consider the system at your place of work and list all the security threats to hardware and software. Indicate those risks that might be accidental and those that could be malicious.

What steps can you take to minimise these risks? Consider procedural steps, such as back-up routines, job specifications, physical locations, extra hardware, passwords, etc.

Explore your back-up procedures.

Activity 4

Copyright law covers:

(a)   reference books, sound recordings, film and broadcasts, computer programs, dramatic and musical works

(b)   books of all kinds, sound recordings, film and broadcasts, computer programs, dramatic and musical works

(c)   books of all kinds, sound recordings, film and broadcasts, computer programs written in the UK, dramatic and musical works

(d)   books of all kinds, sound recordings on CD, film and broadcasts, computer programs, dramatic and musical works.

Which one is correct?

Activity 5

One of your friends at work has told you that she can't remember her password unless it is easy, so she uses her forename, Mary. Can you think of a password that is equally easy but could not be guessed by anyone else?

Activity 6

A small company's computer system comprises five desktop personal computers located in separate offices linked together in a local network within the same building. The computers are not connected to a wide area network and employees are not allowed to take floppy disks into or out of the building. Information that the owner of the business wishes to keep confidential to herself is stored in one of the computers

Which ONE of the following statements can be concluded from this information?

The company's computer system does NOT:

(i)   need a back-up storage system

(ii)   need a password access system

(iii) receive e-mails from customers and suppliers

(iv)   include virus detection software.

Activity 7

Mitchell & Co is a partnership of solicitors. They have five offices situated in various parts of the country.

(a)   What information would you expect to find in their health and safety manual, a copy of which is provided for all new employees?

(b)   What conditions and facilities do you think Mitchell & Co should provide for their employees?

Activity 8

What do you think are the causes of most accidents in the workplace?

Activity 9

Describe your actions in the following situations:

(a)   if you discover a fire

(b)   if you hear the fire alarm.

4

Activity 10

Define the terms:

• Budget

• Variance

Activity 11

Hockeyskill Ltd manufactures hockey sticks and divides its sales function into four main areas:

(1)   Scotland and the North

(2)   Midlands

(3)   South East

(4)   South West.

Its cumulative sales for five months in 20X3 and actual sales for June were:

		Jan–May	June
		£	£
Area	1	31,000	7,100
	2	33,500	8,200
	3	49,000	9,750
	4	41,000	8,210
		£154,500	£33,260

The budget for the six months was:

		£
Area	1	37,500
	2	40,500
	3	57,500
	4	46,500
		£182,000

Prepare a statement for management to show the budget and actual sales for each sales area for the six months ended 30 June showing clearly the variance for each area and in total.

Activity 12

Northcliffe Feeds produces animal feed. It has three main products: A1 Plus, B Plus and Feed Plus. Its planned sales for the quarter ended 30 June 20X3 (budgeted) was:

	Sales tonnes	Selling price per tonne
		£
A1 Plus	12,000	100
B Plus	11,000	120
Feed Plus	9,500	125

Actual sales for the quarter ended 30 June 20X3:

	Sales tonnes	Sales value
		£
A1 Plus	12,600	1,272,600
B Plus	11,000	1,331,000
Feed Plus	9,000	1,116,000

Tasks

- Present a statement to management to show, for each product and in total, the budgeted sales value and the actual sales value and the variance for each.

- Calculate for each product the average actual selling price per tonne.

- Calculate the percentage increase or decrease on the budgeted selling price per tonne per product for the period.

- Present a statement showing for each product and in total the budget and actual tonnage for the period.

Activity 13

The costs of production of a business for the months of April 20X1 and April 20X0 are given below:

	April 20X1	April 20X0
	£	£
Materials	253,400	244,300
Labour	318,200	302,600
Expenses	68,700	72,400

Draw up a table showing the difference between the costs of the current month and of the corresponding month in £s, and as a percentage of the April 20X0 costs.

Activity 14

Given below are the budgeted and actual costs for the two production cost centres of a business for May 20X1.

	Budget	Actual
	£	£
Cost centre 1		
Materials	48,700	46,230
Labour	37,600	39,940
Expenses	5,200	3,700
Cost centre 2		
Materials	56,200	62,580
Labour	22,500	20,400
Expenses	4,800	5,600

You are required to draw up a table showing the amount of the variances for the month. You are also to indicate which variances should be reported to management if it is the business's policy to report only variances that are more than 15% of the budgeted figure.

5

Activity 15

In which example below does the assistant have the authority and ability to delegate to the operatives?

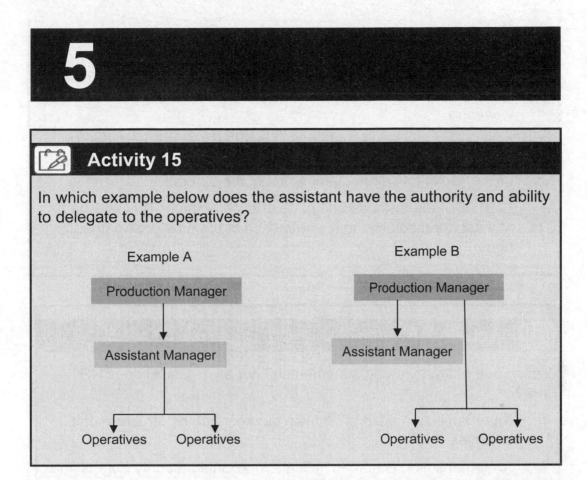

Activity 16

Prepare a checklist of information you would store relating to a meeting at some other organisation's premises

Activity 17

Today is Friday.

Thomas has three tasks to complete, each of which will take two hours. His supervisor is expecting him to have completed them all by 10am on Monday.

Thomas was unable to perform any of the tasks on Friday morning because the computer was not working. It is now 2pm on Friday. Thomas normally goes home at 5pm.

What should Thomas do in these circumstances?

A   Complete one of the tasks and start one of the others. He should be able to complete all of them by noon on Monday.

B   Complete the most urgent task and take home the other two tasks. He is bound to be able to find time to finish them over the weekend.

C   Contact his supervisor immediately and explain the problem. He should suggest that he finishes what he considers to be the most urgent task first before starting one of the others.

D   Start all of the tasks and do parts of each of them. This way he has at least done something towards each of them before he goes home.

Activity 18

Which one of the following statements about an organisation is NOT true?

(i)   An organisation chart provides a summary of the structure of a business.

(ii)   An organisation chart can indicate functional authority but not line authority within a business.

(iii) An organisation chart can improve employees' understanding of their role in a business.

(iv)   An organisation chart can improve internal communications within a business.

KAPLAN PUBLISHING

6

Activity 19

Darren is the supervisor of a travel shop. When his staff take a customer booking, they have to add on a charge for airport taxes. The charges are different for each airport but are found in the company's fares manual.

One afternoon Fiona, who has worked in the shop for six weeks, asks Darren for the charge for Oslo airport. Darren gets angry. What could explain his outburst?

Activity 20

Diana's supervisor is explaining a new accounting procedure to her. Suggest some things that Diana might do which would suggest that she is not listening properly.

How might her supervisor react to these?

Activity 21

Can you think of any advantages and disadvantages associated with the preparation of office manuals?

Activity 22

Your boss is currently overseas negotiating an extension of a sales contract with one of your existing customers. You receive the following fax message from him:

'Urgent – we've agreed that the trade discount applying to the future contracts will be based on a formula related to sales volumes over the last two years. Please fax me the details of monthly sales volumes to this customer over that period immediately.'

Outline the likely consequences if you fail to act quickly on this message.

Activity 23

There are various ways in which a business can communicate information electronically. A facility whereby a duplicate copy of a document can be sent electronically is known as:

(i)   electronic mail or e-mail

(ii)   internet

(iii)   telex

(iv)   facsimile or fax.

KAPLAN PUBLISHING

7

Activity 24

Draw up your own SWOT analysis using the following type of cruciform diagram.

Strengths	Weaknesses
Opportunities	**Threats**

Activity 25

Why are staff appraisals important?

Activity 26

You work in the bought ledger department of a large company – Global Supplies Ltd. The purchasing manager is due to meet a potential new supplier of product PF123. In preparation for the meeting you have been asked to provide an analysis of Global Supplies' purchases of this product over the last few months, showing the unit price charged by two different suppliers the company has used in the past.

(i)   What sources of information would you be likely to access to fulfil this request?

(ii)   The meeting is scheduled for 4pm this Friday coming. It is now 5pm on Wednesday and you have not been able to begin assembling the information because you have had to cover for a colleague who is off sick. You begin to doubt whether you will be able to produce the information on time. What action should you take?

Key Techniques: Answers

3

Activity 1

There are several ways of minimising the risk

- Burglar alarms can be fitted.

- Access to the building can be controlled.

- Smaller items can be locked away securely. Larger pieces of equipment can be bolted to the surface.

- The organisation can maintain a log of all equipment so that its movement can be monitored.

- Disks containing valuable data should not be left lying around.

Activity 2

Examples include:

- Theft of assets, e.g. computers, stock or software.

- Theft of incoming cheques.

- Invented personnel on the payroll.

- Unauthorised discounts given to customers.

- False supplier accounts.

- Corruption and bribery, e.g. when selecting suppliers.

- Abuse of organisation's credit card facilities, e.g. company car fuel allowance privately.

Activity 3

There is no printed answer for this question

Activity 4

The answer is (b)

Activity 5

Using your Christian name may be the easiest way to remember your password, but it will also be easy for someone to gain unauthorised access to your files when you are not at your desk. Alternative passwords that are easy to remember are your mother's maiden name or a brother or sister's name. Try to add in a number e.g. year born, to make it even more difficult for someone to guess it.

Activity 6

(iii)   Because the computers are only connected to a local area network they cannot receive e-mail from customers and suppliers.

KAPLAN PUBLISHING

Activity 7

(a) It would include information on:

(i) the people in charge of health and safety within the firm and their specific responsibilities

(ii) safe operating practices (e.g. the operation of electrical equipment)

(iii) the system for recording accidents in the accident book

(iv) details of first aid available, including the names of qualified first aiders and the position of the first aid box.

(b) Adequate premises which are structurally sound, have adequate fire exits and safety equipment.

Suitable accommodation: suitable temperature, enough space for number of people, proper ventilation, blinds for windows, adequate lighting and safe floor surfaces in good condition.

Appropriate furniture: safety stools to reach items stored on shelves, adjustable chairs for VDU operators and filing cabinets in which only one drawer can be opened at a time.

Adequate toilet and welfare facilities.

Separate accommodation for noisy or dangerous equipment (e.g. photocopiers which give out fumes) or substances (e.g. cleaning materials).

Safe equipment which is serviced regularly by trained technicians.

Activity 8

Most likely causes are:

(a) people tripping up, slipping or falling off equipment or furniture

(b) people being hit by falling objects or colliding with equipment, furniture or other people

(c) people using electrical equipment incorrectly

(d) people using equipment or materials incorrectly.

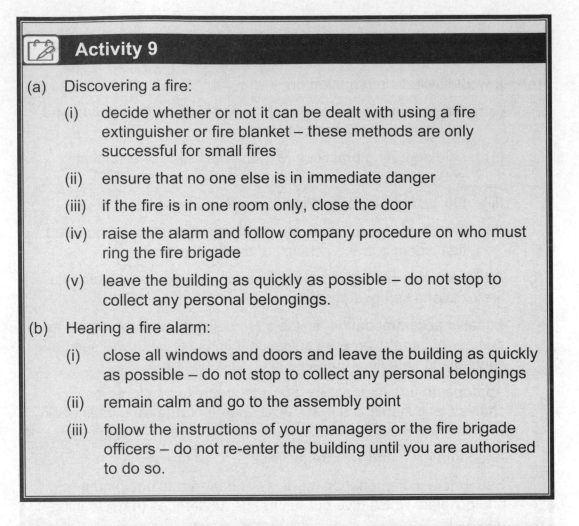

Activity 9

(a) Discovering a fire:

   (i)   decide whether or not it can be dealt with using a fire extinguisher or fire blanket – these methods are only successful for small fires

   (ii)   ensure that no one else is in immediate danger

   (iii) if the fire is in one room only, close the door

   (iv) raise the alarm and follow company procedure on who must ring the fire brigade

   (v)   leave the building as quickly as possible – do not stop to collect any personal belongings.

(b) Hearing a fire alarm:

   (i)   close all windows and doors and leave the building as quickly as possible – do not stop to collect any personal belongings

   (ii)   remain calm and go to the assembly point

   (iii) follow the instructions of your managers or the fire brigade officers – do not re-enter the building until you are authorised to do so.

4

Activity 10

- A budget is forecast figures for costs and income for a future period. Variance:

- The difference between the budget allowance for a level of activity and the actual cost incurred.

Activity 11

Hockeyskill Ltd

Sales report by region

Budget to actual for period ended 30 June

Region	Budget	Actual	Variance F/(A)
	£	£	£
Scotland & North	37,500	38,100	600 F
Midlands	40,500	41,700	1,200 F
South East	57,500	58,750	1,250 F
South West	46,500	49,210	2,710 F
	182,000	187,760	5,760

Activity 12

Northcliffe Feeds Ltd

Sales report by product

Budget to actual period ended 30 June 20X3

Product	Budget value	Actual value	Variance F/(A)
	£	£	£
Al Plus	1,200,000	1,272,600	72,600 F
B Plus	1,320,000	1,331,000	11,000 F
Feed Plus	1,187,500	1,116,000	71,500 A
	3,707,500	3,719,600	12,100 F

Selling price per tonne

	Budget	Actual	% increase (decrease)
		£-p	%
Al Plus	100.00	101.00	1.00
B Plus	120.00	121.00	0.83
Feed Plus	125.00	124.00	(0.80)

Budget and actual sales in tonnes for period ended 30 June 20X3

Product	Budget tonnes	Actual tonnes
Al Plus	12,000	12,600
B Plus	11,000	11,000
Feed Plus	9,500	9,000
	32,500	32,600

Activity 13

	April 20X1 £	April 20X0 £	Difference £	Difference %
Materials	253,400	244,300	9,100	3.7
Labour	318,200	302,600	15,600	5.2
Expenses	68,700	72,400	(3,700)	(5.1)

Activity 14

	Budget £	Actual £	Variance £	Variance %
Cost centre 1				
Materials	48,700	46,230	2,470 fav	5.1
Labour	37,600	39,940	2,340 adv	(6.2)
Expenses	5,200	3,700	1,500 fav	28.8
Cost centre 2				
Materials	56,200	62,580	6,380 adv	(11.4)
Labour	22,500	20,400	2,100 fav	9.3
Expenses	4,800	5,600	800 adv	(16.7)

The two variances which are to be reported to management are the two expense variances.

5

Activity 15

In example A, because the flow of authority is shown as passing down from the production manager to the assistant manager and then on to the operatives. In example B the production manager can delegate to the assistant manager and to the operatives, but the assistant manager is not shown as having any authority over the operators.

Activity 16

Ensure that the following information is included:

(a) the full name and title of the person you intend or are required to see;

(b) the full and precise name and address of the relevant organisation;

(c) the telephone number of the organisation together with the area code (STD code) and the extension of the person you must see;

(d) the time, date and anticipated length of the meeting;

(e) the exact location of the meeting (e.g. which room on which floor in which block);

(f) outline details of the matter to be discussed;

(g) travel directions and details of entrance points and security procedures.

It is, of course, equally important for those details to be sent to people who may be intending to visit you.

Activity 17

C – Contact his supervisor immediately and explain the problem. He should suggest that he finishes what he considers to be the most urgent task first before starting one of the others.

Activity 18

(ii)   is not true because an organisation chart does indicate line authority within a business.

6

Activity 19

Darren might be used to giving his staff this information (particularly as Fiona is a new employee) but on this day one of the following may apply:

(a)   he is very busy himself

(b)   he has personal problems.

He might expect all staff to look up information for themselves and several other people might already have asked him.

Activity 20

Diana might:

(a)   look away or out of the window

(b)   play with a pencil or other item

(c)   continue writing

(d)   interrupt unnecessarily.

Her supervisor might assume that she is either not capable of doing the job or not interested. Her supervisor might decide not to give her some more interesting work as a type of punishment.

Activity 21

The advantages and disadvantages associated with the preparation of office manuals include:

Advantages

(i) To prepare an office manual the systems and procedures must be examined carefully. This close attention can only benefit the organisation, in that strengths and weaknesses are revealed.

(ii) Supervision is easier.

(iii) It helps the induction and training of new staff.

(iv) It helps to pinpoint areas of responsibility.

(v) Having been written down in the first place, systems and procedures are easier to adapt and/or change in response to changing circumstances.

Disadvantages

(i) There is an associated expense in preparing manuals both in the obvious financial terms and the perhaps less obvious cost of administrative time.

(ii) To be of continuing use an office manual must be updated periodically, again incurring additional expense.

(iii) The instructions as laid down in the office manual may be interpreted rather strictly and implemented too rigidly. Within any organisation it is often beneficial for employees to bring a degree of flexibility to their duties to cope with particular circumstances.

Activity 22

(i) Your boss would look foolish and the customer will have a poor opinion of your organisation's efficiency.

(ii) Without detailed and accurate information to base the discounts on, your boss may be forced to defer discussions until a later, and perhaps less opportune, occasion. Alternatively, he could concede an over-generous rate of discount to finalise the deal while he has the opportunity.

(iii) Your boss will form a poor opinion of your abilities and reliability, with possible damaging consequences to your later career.

Activity 23

(iv) A facsimile or fax is a facility for sending a duplicate copy of a document electronically.

7

Activity 24

There is no printed answer for this question.

Activity 25

The appraisal is important in staff counselling and development. This would involve such matters as:

- Feedback on performance and problems encountered – they establish an individual's current level of performance and identify strengths and weaknesses.

- Career development – they identify training and development needs.

- Identifying job interests and likely development areas – they can motivate individuals.

- Defining performance targets – they provide a basis for rewarding staff in relation to their contribution to organisational goals.

- Reviewing promotion potential – they assess potential and provide information for succession planning.

- Enabling individuals to appreciate where their jobs fit in the overall company scheme.

KAPLAN PUBLISHING

Activity 26

(i)   Possible sources of information include:

   (a)   the bought ledger accounts of the two current suppliers

   (b)   invoices from the two current suppliers

   (c)   costing records showing purchasing costs over the last six months.

(ii) You should immediately contact the purchasing manager and explain the problem. It may be possible to take action to salvage the meeting by asking for help from someone who has not such a heavy workload. Alternatively, the meeting may be postponed.

PROJECT
QUESTIONS and ANSWERS

Project: Questions

Scenario

Your name is Katie Smith and you started working for Tip Top Fitness on 24th April 20X1.

Today's date is 26th May 20X1.

Tip Top Fitness are a company that manufacture and sell fitness equipment to gyms. The Sales Team at Tip Top Fitness attend fitness conventions where they are able to demonstrate and sell equipment; they also hire fitness professionals to help demonstrate this equipment.

The Accounts Department is split into two sections:

Financial Accounts – nominal ledger, sales ledger, purchase ledger and tax records

Management Accounts – stocks and regional management accounts

You are contracted to work 9.00 to 17.00, five days per week. You are also required to take a one hour lunch break.

If you need to work longer you can work an extra hour overtime without requesting permission. Any further overtime would require you request permission from Paul Cadwell the Financial Accountant.

You spent the first day at Tip Top Fitness having an induction into the company. Paul Cadwell introduced you to everybody who worked in the accounts department and went through all of the emergency procedures and company policies with you. The policies you received are listed below:

- Expenses Policy
- Freelance Payment Policy
- Equal Opportunities and Diversity Policy
- Health and Safety Policy
- Grievance Procedure
- Your Job Description and Person Specification

Your job role is to assist the accountants in the Financial Accounts Department. You may be required to assist in some tasks for other departments if required. You will report directly to Paul Cadwell.

See organisation chart on page 215.

Any person requiring you to assist them must submit a work request form to you prior to 11am on a Friday. This ensures that you have time to check that you are able to complete the tasks and also give you time to plan your work schedule for the following week. You must keep two hours free on a Friday to plan the following weeks work.

Any work requests submitted to you after that time must be signed off by Paul Cadwell, Head of Financial Accounts.

Paul Cadwell has requested that you keep a copy of all the requests and issues that have arisen in your first month at Tip Top Fitness. He explained that any tasks that you don't understand can be gone through fully at your first month review and any extra training required can then be planned.

As part of your job role you will be required to calculate some costs on any staff training and development. Your AAT course will be included in this. Paul Cadwell authorises all the payments for staff training and development and is also the person who will be involved in your own training with your AAT course.

Organisational chart

Tip Top Fitness – Accounts Department

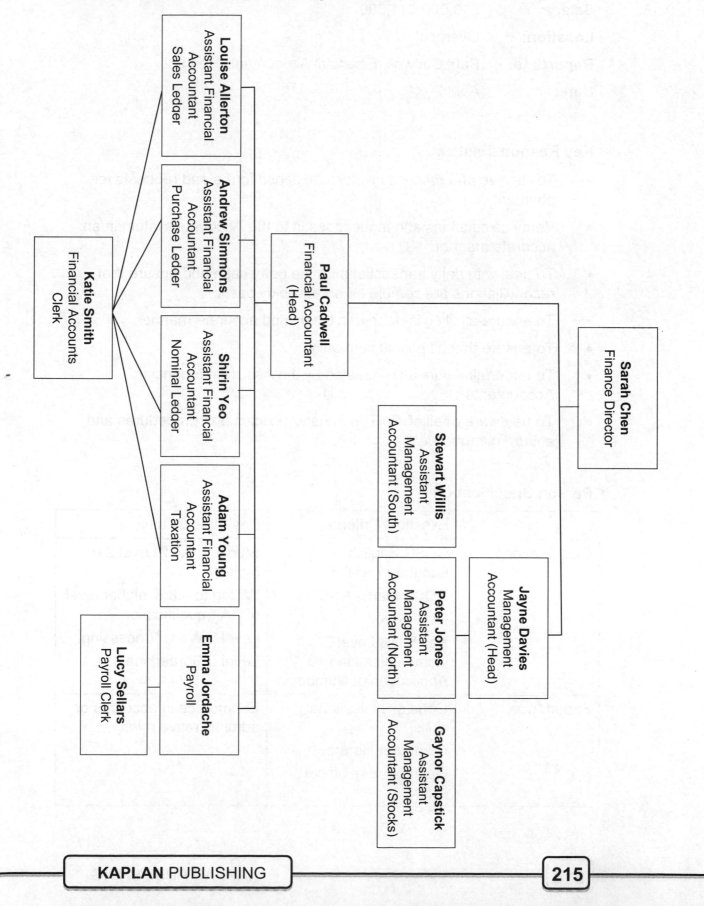

Job Description

Job Title: Financial Accounts Clerk

Salary: £10,000-£11,500

Location: Liverpool

Reports to: Paul Cadwell, Financial Accountant (Head)

Date: April 20X1

Key Responsibilities

- To receive and process invoices, expense forms and requests for payment.

- Verify calculations and input codes in to the Accounts system in an accurate manner.

- To deal with daily transactions for the petty cash and ensure that reconciliations are completed on a weekly basis.

- To ensure all filing is done in a timely and accurate manner.

- To ensure that all post is sent daily.

- To undertake work as requested by the Assistant Financial Accountants

- To be aware of all of Tip Top Fitness' policies and procedures and ensure compliance.

Person Specification

	Essential Criteria	Desirable Criteria
Qualifications	GCSE English Language A*-C GCSE Maths A*-C Or Key Skills Level 2 Communication and Application of Number	Studying AAT Level 2 or higher Willing to study higher level of AAT qualification. Level 2 Word Processing. Level 2 Spreadsheets.
Experience	Good organisational skills. Computer literate. Good general office skills.	Experience in accounts or administrative role.

Communication Skills	Excellent communication skills, including: Telephone, Email, Letter and face to face. Ability to communicate to groups of people. A good understanding of confidentiality.	
Teamwork	The ability to work flexibly. Knowledge and understanding of team working.	Experience of team working.

Grievance Procedure

Introduction

Tip Top Fitness' aim is to ensure that employees with a grievance relating to their employment can use a procedure which can help to resolve grievances as quickly and as fairly as possible.

Informal discussions

If an employee has a grievance about their employment they should discuss it informally with an immediate supervisor. We hope that the majority of concerns will be resolved this way.

Stage 1 – statement of grievance

If the employee feels that the matter has not been resolved through informal discussions, they should put your grievance in writing to an immediate supervisor.

Stage 2 – the grievance meeting

Within 5 working days the supervisor will respond, in writing, to the statement, inviting the employee to attend a meeting where the alleged grievance can be discussed. This meeting should be scheduled to take place as soon as possible and normally 5 working days notice of this meeting will be provided to the employee and they will be informed of their right to be accompanied.

Employees must take all reasonable steps to attend the meeting, but if for any unforeseen reason the employee, or the employer, can't attend, the meeting must be rearranged.

After the meeting the supervisor hearing the grievance must write to the employee informing them of any decision or action and offering them the right of appeal. This letter should be sent within 5 working days of the grievance meeting and should include the details on how to appeal.

Step 3 – appeal

If the matter is not resolved to the employees' satisfaction they must set out their grounds of appeal in writing within 5 working days of receipt of the decision letter.

Within 5 working days of receiving an appeal letter, the employee should receive a written invitation to attend an appeal meeting. The appeal meeting should be taken by a more senior manager not involved in the original meeting.

After the appeal meeting with senior manager must inform the employee in writing of their decision within 5 working days of the meeting. Their decision is final.

Freelance Payment Policy

Freelance Instructors are to be paid flat rates of £100 per day or £50 per half day. Expenses are also available on production of receipts.

Invoices must be submitted before 24th of each month to ensure payment at the end of the same month.

Any invoices submitted to accounts on the 25th or later will not be paid until the following month.

It is the sales teams' responsibility to ensure that invoices are submitted before 24th of the month. It is also the sales teams' responsibility to inform freelance instructors should they miss the cut off date.

Accounts Overtime Policy

The Accounts at Tip Top Fitness are split into two departments, Financial Accounts and Management Accounts.

Each department are contracted to work 9.00 to 17.00, Monday to Friday with an hour lunch which must be taken. Both departments are open from 8.00 to 18.00. Staff are allowed to work one hour overtime per day to complete work if necessary without requiring permission from the heads of department.

Any staff member who feels they need to work more than the one hour must get permission from the department head for the overtime. Without this permission staff will not be paid for the overtime worked.

All overtime is checked regularly to ensure that staff are not working unnecessary overtime.

Work Request Forms

WORK REQUEST FORM: Katie Smith		Date: 26 May 20X1	
From: Louise Allerton			
Code	Task	Est Time	Deadline
LA1	Analyse prepayments and provide report	4 hours	31 May
LA2	Reconcile stock figures with lists from Management Accounts.	4 hours	12pm 1 June
LA3	Check list from Management Accounts and action adjustments.	3 hours	1pm 1 June
LA4	Collect sales enquiries, cash payments and invoice details from Sales Team from weekend and record.	3 hours	2 June
LA5	Collect donations from everyone in the Accounts Department for Peter Jones' leaving present	2 hours	2 June

WORK REQUEST FORM: Katie Smith		Date: 26 May 20X1	
From: Andrew Simmons			
Code	Task	Est Time	Deadline
AS1	Complete payments to freelance instructors and record on system.	3 hours	30 May
AS2	Check supplier statements against purchase ledger balances and record any differences.	3 hours	1 June

WORK REQUEST FORM: Katie Smith		Date: 26 May 20X1	
From: Shirin Yeo			
Code	Task	Est Time	Deadline
SY1	Contact debtors from attached list and request payment ASAP. Update debtor records with outcome.	6 hours	31 May
SY2	Complete banking documentation for attached cheques from debtors	4 hours	31 May
SY3	Provide report with outcome of debtor conversations for meeting.	2 hours	2 June

WORK REQUEST FORMS: Katie Smith		Date: 26 May 20X1	
From: Sales Team			
Code	Task	Est Time	Deadline
ST1	Provide report of payments made to freelance instructors for January-April for Sales Meeting on Monday.	3 hours	1pm 29 May

Continual Professional Development (CPD)

Paul Cadwell has provided you with the following CPD requests for **July to December 20X1**

Name	Event/Course	Provider/ Organisation	Duration	Cost
Louise Allerton	AAT Level 4	Kaplan	1 day per month July-Sept 4 days in Nov and 2 days Dec	£2,000
	VAT update	HMRC	1 day	Free
	AAT Membership	AAT	N/A	£74
	AAT Exam Entry × 3	AAT	N/A	£141
	Legal compliance	Local Branch	1 day	£300
Andrew Simmons	Legal compliance	Local Branch	1 day	£300
	VAT update	HMRC	1 day	Free
Shirin Yeo	ACCA Final Level	Kaplan	1 day per month starting in September	£2,000
	Managing People and Delegation	Local Branch	1 day	£250
Adam Young	CTA Qualification – Distance Learning	Kaplan	6 days (study leave and assessments)	£3,000
	VAT update	HMRC	1 day	Free
	On line Reporting	HMRC	1 day	Free
	Income Tax update	HMRC	1 day	Free

Name	Event/Course	Provider/ Organisation	Duration	Cost
Emma Jordache	AAT Level 4	Kaplan	1 day per month July-Sept 4 days in Nov and 2 days Dec	£2,000
	HMRC payroll update	HMRC	1 day	Free
Lucy Sellars	AAT Payroll Level 3	Kaplan	1 afternoon per month July-Dec	£1,250
	HMRC payroll update	HMRC	1 day	Free
Katie Smith	AAT Level 2	Kaplan	1 day per month July-Sept	£1,400

Costs for covering work of staff attending formal training.

Assistant Financial Accountant/Payroll Manager grade - £55 per half day

Clerk grade - £35 per half day

Overtime paid for evening courses is equivalent to half day pay for the grade.

1

Task 1.1

The accounts department does not work in isolation at Tip Top Fitness. Information needs to flow to and from the department to help the company run.

(a) **Give two examples of the type of work the accounts department do at Tip Top Fitness.**

(b) **To complete your work in accounts you will require information from the other departments at Tip Top Fitness. Give two examples and explain how you use this information.**

(c) **Explain how this information can help Tip Top Fitness fun efficiently and help maintain its solvency.**

Also explain what sort of legal legislation must be observed when completing this work.

Task 1.2

A couple of issues have arisen concerning work you need to complete and with your AAT study.

(a) **You have a problem with a sales invoice. Who do you need to speak to resolve this issue?**

(b) **You require some study leave to prepare for an AAT exam. Who would you need to discuss this with?**

Task 1.3

Tip Top Fitness occasionally employs Freelance Fitness Presenters to demonstrate their products at showcase events.

The Sales Team received an invoice on Saturday 20th May 20X1 and sent it over to you on Friday 26th May for payment at end May 20X1.

Referring to the Freelance Payment Policy on page 6, write an email to the head of the sales department with any issues you have and the consequences of those issues.

To:	
From:	
Date:	
Subject:	

Task 1.4

As part of your Friday afternoon tasks you receive work requests from the other members of the accounts team and occasionally the Head of Sales, you then plan your next week's work schedule.

(a) **Using the work requests, complete the work schedule below. Refer to the Overtime Policy on page 7 if you feel you need to.**

	Monday 29	Tuesday 30	Wednesday 31	Thursday 1	Friday 2
8am					
9am					
10am					
11am					
12pm					
1pm	Lunch	Lunch	Lunch	Lunch	Lunch
2pm	STUDY LEAVE				
3pm	STUDY LEAVE				PLAN WORK
4pm	STUDY LEAVE				PLAN WORK
O/T if required					

(b) **If you have any problems with deadlines then please explain to whom you would speak to and what you may be able to do to rectify the problem.**

Task 1.5

Paul Cadwell has agreed that you can take study leave on the Monday afternoon as long as any required tasks for that day are completed.

After completing your work schedule for the following week Adam Young comes to you and asks that you do some work for him on the Monday morning.

(a) **Explain to him why you cannot complete this work and what the implications would be if you did not complete your scheduled work.**

| |
| |
| |
| |
| |
| |
| |

(b) Adam is upset that you will not do the work for him as he feels that he has not asked you to do as much work the following week as some of the other members of staff have.

Adam tries to pressure you not to take your study leave and to complete his work instead by saying that he will miss his child's school play and that he did not think it was fair that you have study leave when he never did for his AAT course.

How would you try to resolve this issue first?

If you could not resolve this issue what would you do?

2

 Task 2.1

Part of your job role is to analyse the CPD requests of the accounts department.

Using the CPD Request Sheet, calculate:

(a)   **The total cost to be paid to training providers per member of staff and as a whole.**

(b)   **The cost of any cover or overtime required to be paid for people on courses.**

(c)   **The complete cost of all the CPD training.**

(d)   **The cost for each employee as a percentage (to 2 decimal places) of the total cost of CPD.**

Show all of your workings out:

KAPLAN PUBLISHING

Task 2.2

All of the accounts department are members of either ACCA, CIMA or AAT. Fred Smith from Head Office (Quarry Lane, Milton, ML10 3PT) has asked you to write to him explaining why they need to be members and why they require further training even though they are qualified. Include why CPD is important.

Tip Top Fitness
Switch Road
Liverpool
LL33 9BP

26th May 20X1

Activity 2.3

It is almost time for you to have your first work review with Paul Cadwell. Before the review he has asked you to identify any training you feel you require so he can discuss it with you at the review.

(a) Using the Job description and Person Specification identify two strengths and weaknesses you feel you have.

STRENGTHS	WEAKNESSES

(b) Using your identified weaknesses and your career aspirations complete a Personal Development Plan.

Identify at least four development needs.

What do I want/need to learn?	What will I do to achieve this learning need?	What resources or support will I need?	Target date for completion	With whom and when this will be reviewed
1. AAT Level 2 Certificate in Accounting	Attend college	Time to study for my exams	July 20X1	Paul Cadwell at three month review
2.				
3.				
4.				
5.				
6.				

(c)   Finally, before your meeting Paul Cadwell would like you to write a report which reviews your first month at Tip Top Fitness.

Include:

- An overview of your first month.

- Any difficulties you encountered and how you resolved them.

- How you produced your PDP, what documents did you use to analyse your strengths and weaknesses?

- Why it is important to review your PDP regularly.

Report:
To:
From:
Date:

Project: Suggested Answers

1

Task 1.1

(a) Give two examples of the type of work the accounts department do at Tip Top Fitness.

The accounts department would complete various tasks such as process invoices, process expense claims, salary and overtime hours, prepare month and year end accounts and produce current costs against the expected budgeted costs.

(b) To complete your work in accounts you will require information from the other departments at Tip Top Fitness. Give two examples and explain how you use this information.

The accounts department receives information for all the other departments in a company. A few examples are invoices received to process and pay, expense claims, salary and overtimes hours for payroll and also any changes to staff details.

(c) Explain how information provided by the accounts department can help Tip Top Fitness run efficiently and help maintain its solvency.

Also explain what sort of legal legislation must be observed when completing this work.

The accounts department can provide information to other departments on how efficiently they are running and if there are any improvements that can be done.

They will also produce annual budgets and during the year will provide actual figures which can be compared to the budgets to again ensure efficiency. Information on debtors and having strict credit control policies in place will ensure that the cash balances of Tip Top are monitored and therefore solvency can be assured.

Health and Safety, Data Protection, Employment Law and Corporate Requirements.

Task 1.2

(a) **You have a problem with a sales invoice. Who do you need to speak to resolve this issue?**

If I had any issues with sales invoices I would refer them to Louise Allerton who is the Assistant Financial Accountant, Sales Ledger.

(b) **You require some study leave to prepare for an AAT exam. Who would you need to discuss this with?**

Paul Cadwell the Financial Accountant is responsible for authorising staff training and he is also responsible for my training with the AAT

Task 1.3

The Sales Team received an invoice on Saturday 20th May 20X1 and sent it over to you on Friday 26th May for payment at end May 20X1.

Referring to the Freelance Payment Policy on page 6, write an email to the head of the sales department with any issues you have and the consequences of those issues.

To:	paul.jones@tip-top-fitness.co.uk
From:	katie.smith@tip-top-fitness.co.uk
Date:	26/05/20X1
Subject:	Freelance Invoice dated 20th May 20X1

Hi Paul,

I am emailing you with an issue regarding an invoice for a freelance payment, which I have received today, to process for payment.

The invoice is dated Saturday 20th May 20X1 and if it was submitted the following Monday would have been processed for payment at the end of this month.

Unfortunately, this invoice has only just been submitted. The cut off date for freelance payments to be paid at month end is 25th of the month. As this invoice was only submitted today, then I am afraid this payment will not now go through until next month. Could you please inform the freelancer that payment will not be made until the end of June.

I would appreciate it if you could inform the sales team that all invoices must be submitted by the 25th of the month for payment that month.

Regards

Katie Smith, Financial Accounts Clerk

Task 1.4

(a) **Using the work requests, complete the work schedule below. Refer to the Overtime Policy on page 184 if you feel you need to.**

	Monday 29	Tuesday 30	Wednesday 31	Thursday 1	Friday 2
8am	ST1	AS1	SY1	LA2	LA4
9am	ST1	LA1	SY1	LA2	LA4
10am	ST1	LA1	SY1	LA3	SY3
11am	AS1	LA1	SY2	LA3	SY3
12pm	AS1	LA1	SY2	LA3	LA5
1pm	Lunch	Lunch	Lunch	Lunch	Lunch
2pm	STUDY LEAVE	SY1	SY2	AS2	LA5
3pm	STUDY LEAVE	SY1	SY2	AS2	PLAN WORK
4pm	STUDY LEAVE	SY1	LA2	AS2	PLAN WORK
O/T if required			LA2	LA4	

(b) **If you have any problems with deadlines then please explain to whom you would speak to and what you may be able to do to rectify the problem.**

I would firstly speak to the person who has requested the work from me and explain that I may struggle to reach a deadline for the work that they have given me.

If I was able to meet the deadline by working overtime, I would speak to Paul Cadwell, who is the head of the department and has the authority to authorise any overtime required.

KAPLAN PUBLISHING

Task 1.5

(a) **Explain to him why you cannot complete this work and what the implications would be if you did not complete your scheduled work.**

As Adam Young had approached me after the cut off time for work requests, I would

explain to him that I completed my work schedule for the following week and that I have also had to have extra overtime authorised to be able to complete the work.

I would explain to him that by accepting his job then a number of other jobs would end up being delayed and the deadlines for these jobs missed.

(b) **Adam is upset that you will not do the work for him as he feels that he has not asked you to do as much work the following week as some of the other members of staff have.**

Adam tries to pressure you not to take your study leave and to complete his work instead by saying that he will miss his child's school play and that he did not think it was fair that you have study leave when he never did for his AAT course.

How would you try to resolve this issue first?

I would speak to Adam and suggest that we discuss deadlines for jobs with the other members of the accounts department to see if any of these deadlines could be moved, so that I could complete Adam's work without missing any other deadlines.

If you could not resolve this issue what would you do?

If this did not resolve the issue then I would suggest that Paul Cadwell be brought into the discussions to see if a satisfactory solution could be found.

2

Task 2.1

(a) **The total cost to be paid to training providers per member of staff and as a whole.**

(b) **The cost of any cover or overtime required to be paid for people on courses.**

(c) **The complete cost of all the CPD training.**

(d) **The cost for each employee as a percentage (to 2 decimal places) of the total cost of CPD.**

Show all of your workings out:

a. LA: 2,000 + 74 + 141 + 300 = 2,515   AS: 300

 SY: 2,000 + 250 = 2,250   AY: 3,000

 EJ: 2,000   LS: 1,250   KS: 1,400

 Total: 2,515 + 300 + 2,250 + 3,000 + 2,000 + 1,250 + 1,400 = 12,715

b. LA: 11 days @ (55 × 2) = 1,210   AS: 2 days @ (55 × 2) = 220

 SY: 5 days @ (55 × 2) = 550   AY: 9 days @ (55 × 2) = 990

 EJ: 10 days @ (55 × 2) = 1,100   LS: 4 days @ (35 × 2) = 280

 KS: 3 days @ (35 × 2) = 210

 Total: 1,210 + 220 + 550 + 990 + 1,100 + 280 + 210 = 4,560

c. 12,715 + 4,560 = 17,275

d. LA: 2,515 + 1,210 = 3,725   (3,725 / 17,275) × 100 = 21.56%

 AS: 300 + 220 = 520   (520 / 17,275) × 100 = 3.01%

 SY: 2,250 + 550 = 2800   (2,800 / 17,275) × 100 = 16.21%

 AY: 3,000 + 990 = 3,990   (3,990 / 17,275) × 100 = 23.10%

 EJ: 2,000 + 1,100 = 3,100   (3,100 / 17,275) × 100 = 17.95%

 LS: 1,250 + 280 = 1,530   (1,530 / 17,275) × 100 = 8.86%

 KS: 1,400 = 210 = 1,610   (1,610 / 17,275) × 100 = 9.32%

Task 2.2

Tip Top Fitness
Switch Road
Liverpool
LL33 9BP

Fred Smith
Tip Top Fitness Head Office
Quarry Lane
Milton
ML10 3PT

26th May 20X1

Dear Fred

CPD for the Accounting Department

I replying to your query concerning the Accounts Department CPD. Specifically, why they are doing further even though they are qualified.

All of Tip Top Fitness' Accounts Department employees are members of professional bodies and these bodies require that their members ensure their technical knowledge is up to date. This is done through courses, master classes, training, conferences and branch meetings, amongst other things. These are collectively known as Continual Professional Development.

As a company Tip Top Fitness will also benefit be ensuring their staff's knowledge is up to date, which would also ensure that regulatory standards are being met. It also ensures that Tip Top Fitness will be working more efficiently and more likely to remain solvent. CPD will also increase the employees' knowledge of new areas, this will also benefit Tip Top Fitness as the staff may be able to undertake further work.

I hope this fully explains the need for CPD within the accounts department at Tip Top Fitness but if you do have any further queries, then please do not hesitate to contact me.

Your Sincerely

Katie Smith

Financial Accounts Clerk
Tip Top Fitness

Task 2.3

(a) **Using the Job description and Person Specification identify two strengths and weaknesses you feel you have.**

STRENGTHS	WEAKNESSES

Students should assess their own skills against those identified in the person specification and also the requirements column of the job description.

(b) **Using your identified weaknesses and your career aspirations complete a Personal Development Plan.**

Identify at least four development needs.

Students should make sensible suggestions related to the role of Katie Smith and also use their own career aspirations. Sensible timescales should be considered.

(c) **Finally, before your meeting Paul Cadwell would like you to write a report which reviews your first month at Tip Top Fitness.**

Include:

- **An overview of your first month.**

- **Any difficulties you encountered and how you resolved them.**

- **How you produced your PDP, what documents did you use to analyse your strengths and weaknesses?**

- **Why it is important to review your PDP regularly.**

Report: First Month Progress

To: Paul Cadwell

From: Katie Smith

Date: 26th May 20X1

Review of First Month

Students should talk about their first month including their induction and what they were told (policies and procedures and reporting structures).

Difficulties

Students should mention the problem with the work schedule with Adam Young and how they resolved the issue.

Personal Development Plan

Students should discuss how they analysed their strengths and weaknesses and what documents they used to produce the results.

PDP

Students need to discuss how their progress should be monitored so that the management of Tip Top Fitness can assess their development needs.

INDEX